HISTORIC MAPS AND VIEWS OF
LONDON

GEORGE SINCLAIR

*Historische
Karten und Ansichten
von London*

*Cartes et
vues historiques
de Londres*

Copyright © 2009 Black Dog and Leventhal Publishers
ISBN: 978-1-57912-797-8

Cover and interior design by Toshiya Masuda

Image credits:
© Alfred Daniels 23
© akg-images 7; © British Library 20
Art Resource, NY © HIP 1, 9; © The Stapleton Collection 14
Author's Private Collection 18
The Bridgeman Art Library © Private Collection / The Stapleton Collection 2; © Guildhall Library, City of London, 5, 10, 21;
© City of Westminster Archive Centre, London, UK, 13; © Private Collection, 19
Corbis © Stapleton Collection 8; © The Gallery Collection 11, 17; © Swim Ink 2, LLC 22
© Getty Images 15
© Max Roberts 24
© Museum of London 3, 4, 6, 12, 16

All rights reserved. No part of this book, either text or illustration, may be used or reproduced in any form without prior written permission from the publisher.

© **2010 for this edition: Tandem Verlag GmbH**
h.f.ullmann is an imprint of Tandem Verlag GmbH

Editors: Hannah Schweizer, Harro Schweizer
Translation to German: Susanne Claussen
Translation to French: Laurence Wuillemin
Typesetting: Prill Partners producing, Berlin
Project coordination: Swetlana Dadaschewa
Overall responsibility for production: h.f.ullmann publishing, Potsdam, Germany

Printed in China

ISBN: 978-3-8331-5771-4

10 9 8 7 6 5 4 3 2 1
X IX VIII VII VI V IV III II I

If you would like to be informed about forthcoming h.f.ullmann titles, you can request
our newsletter by visiting our website (**www.ullmann-publishing.com**) or by emailing us at:
newsletter@ullmann-publishing.com.
h.f.ullmann, Birkenstraße 10, 14469 Potsdam, Germany

INTRODUCTION

Maps have existed since the time of the ancient Egyptians. Even Alexander the Great (356–323 BC) had mapmakers who accompanied him on his campaigns. The Greek geographer Strabo (born c. 63 BC) produced *Geographia*, a collection of seventeen books describing the geographical scope of Europe, Asia, and Africa. The collection comprises his own observations, historical material, and descriptions of places he had seen and people he had met during his travels.

Although many of these books survived, most maps produced during this time did unfortunately not, and it was not until the fifteenth century that maps really began to be preserved. Although London was established by the Romans 2,000 years ago, very few original maps or views of the city exist before 1500. Much of the city during this period was contained within an area measuring one mile by one mile with many people living outside the city walls in small villages and farming communities.

Since the sixteenth century, due to the pressure of economic conditions, social change, technological advancements, the domination of Europe through its supremacy of the oceans, the colonization of foreign lands, and the political power of the city of London over the rest of Great Britain, London has outgrown its boundaries time and time again. Villages and settlements were absorbed into the capital to eventually form the home countries and, subsequently, the boroughs of Greater London, stretching some fifteen to twenty miles from the center of the city. For four hundred years, people have been asking the same questions, which remain of special urgency today: how big is London, and where does London stop?

These and other similar questions have been answered, in part, by the map. In the early days, it was Dutch and German engravers, with their engraving and printing expertise, who published maps of London. The first known full-scale map of London was produced around 1550 by a cartographer thought to be Anthony van den Wyngaerde. Unfortunately only a fragment exists of a version engraved on copperplate and a woodcut derivative.

The first full map of London to survive is an engraving by Frans Hogenberg that was published in 1572. This map depicts London just before the reign of Queen Elizabeth I, at a time when the City of London had a population of about 75,000.

Although a number of panoramic drawings and views of London were produced in the first half of the seventeenth century, it was the Great Fire of London in 1666 that provided the next great impetus to create maps, plans, and views of the city. The fire raged for five days, destroying more than 13,000 houses and 89 churches (including St. Paul's Cathedral), and covered an area of 420 acres. Eighty percent of the City of London was destroyed and 80,000 people were evacuated.

During the reconstruction of the city, the roads were widened and solid brick buildings were erected (prior to the fire, many of the houses and public buildings were constructed of highly flammable wood and tar). Of course, new maps and plans had to be drawn as the rebuilding of London continued over many years under the direction of the head of the Commission for the Rebuilding of London, Sir Christopher Wren.

During the early part of the eighteenth century, very few maps of the city were produced, and those that were reprints or new editions of old maps or were imported from Holland, where most of the printing in Europe was being done at that time. However, in 1712, a duty of 30 percent was imposed on imported maps, and thereafter the production of London maps returned gradually to London publishers.

The Rocque family, immigrants from France, embarked on an ambitious plan to survey the entire City of London. The map took nine years to complete, was divided into squares and numbered for reference, and included an index of the streets. It was published in 1746 and became the standard format for future city maps.

During the nineteenth century, many new elegant houses and public buildings were erected, first by the Georgians and continuing through the Regency period and the era of Queen Victoria, as were new roads, canals, tramways, and railways. The ever-changing face of London resulted, again, in the need for new maps and plans for the citizens and the many visitors to the city.

Detailed maps were produced for the Metropolitan Police, formed in 1829, covering the city to the outskirts and eventually including all parishes within fifteen miles of the capital (the area that became known as Greater London). Many maps detailing the sewers and tunnels of the city, as well as the waterworks, waterways (canals), and rivers, were drawn by city authorities. Maps were also produced to identify the boroughs of London – some even showed the political leanings or wealth of the city.

Transportation became a key factor in the growth of London and, as such, the need for transport maps grew steadily. Route maps of the railway, steam tramways, and horse-drawn buses became essential once these services were introduced in Victorian London, and again for the Electric Railways (now the Underground or Tube) when they were introduced in 1863.

London and its environment has always been of great interest to engravers and publishers and has been the fascination of historians, illustrators, and painters who either lived in the capital or were visitors to this famous city. Oil paintings came into vogue in the sixteenth century, when the royal and wealthy families commissioned portraits of their relatives and likenesses of their estates to hang on their walls, as well as depictions of the great buildings of London and other historic places of recognition.

Many of the drawings, engravings, and lithographs on the history of London were produced for books and for magazines and newspapers of the day (such as the *Illustrated London News*, *The Times of London* and *Vanity Fair*). Paintings and drawings of London also served to emphasize that the city had become the established political center of England because of its financial and commercial power. The Thames River was a symbol of that power, and there are several images in this collection that depict the river as a thriving hub of business through its dockyards, wharfs, barges, markets, and manufacturing industry.

Whereas the Great Fire of London was the catalyst for the redevelopment and growth of medieval London, it was the devastation caused during World War II that was ultimately responsible for the current shape and architecture of modern London. Between 1940 and 1941, London was heavily bombed by the German air force in an effort to cripple the city's financial industry, transport services, shipping channels, and the movement of goods in and out of the city. Much of the center of London was destroyed and had to be rebuilt. The contemporary painting by Alfred Daniels, "Lambeth Palace and the House of Commons", captures London as it looks today, the Thames now serene and serving London mainly as a tourist attraction.

These days the invention of commercial photography has taken over as the popular format for capturing views of the city. Most modern maps of London are practical guides for getting people from one part of town to another or for traveling through the city to specific destinations, and visitors to London are easily recognizable as they pore over printed maps of the city or the Underground.

EINLEITUNG

Die Erstellung von Landkarten geht bis in die Zeit der alten Ägypter zurück, und auch schon Alexander der Große (356–323 v. Chr.) wurde auf seinen Feldzügen von Kartografen begleitet. Der griechische Geograf Strabo (um 63 v. Chr. geboren) erstellte eine aus siebzehn Büchern bestehende Sammlung, die *Geographia*, die geografische Informationen über Europa, Asien und Afrika enthält. Die Sammlung umfasst neben seinen eigenen Beobachtungen auch historische Informationen über Orte, Menschen und Kulturen seiner Zeit, die er auf Reisen sammeln konnte.

Obgleich die Bände der Sammlung erhalten sind, existieren die meisten Landkarten leider nicht mehr, da erst im 15. Jahrhundert eine Konservierung der Landkarten vorgenommen wurde. Obwohl London bereits vor 2000 Jahren von den Römern gegründet wurde, gibt es nur noch wenige Karten oder Ansichten der Stadt aus der Zeit vor 1500. Der Großteil der Stadt befand sich in einem 2,5 Quadratkilometer großen Gebiet. Ein bedeutender Bevölkerungsanteil lebte außerhalb der Stadtmauern in kleinen Ortschaften und bäuerlichen Dörfern.

Aufgrund der veränderten Wirtschaftsbedingungen, des gesellschaftlichen Wandels, der technologischen Fortschritte, der Vorherrschaft Europas auf den Meeren und der Kolonisierung fremder Länder wuchs London seit dem 16. Jahrhundert kontinuierlich über seine bestehenden Grenzen hinaus. Die Hauptstadt verleibte sich Dörfer und Ansiedlungen ein und machte sie zu heimischen Bezirken, aus denen später wiederum die Stadtteile Londons entstanden. Vom Stadtzentrum aus gesehen erstreckte sich das Gebiet nun über 25 bis dreißig Kilometer stadtauswärts. Seit nunmehr vierhundert Jahren stellen sich die Menschen immer wieder dieselbe Frage, die sich auch heute noch aufdrängt: Wie groß ist London eigentlich, und wo endet es?

Diese und ähnliche Fragen werden zum Teil durch Karten beantwortet. Anfangs waren es die holländischen und deutschen Graveure, die ihre Fachkenntnisse in der Gravurkunst und Drucktechnik nutzten, um Karten von London zu erstellen. Die erste bekannte maßstabsgetreue Karte Londons wurde um 1550 vermutlich von dem Kartografen Anthony van den Wyngaerde erstellt. Bedauerlicherweise sind nur Fragmente einer auf einer Kupferplatte gravierten Version und ein Holzmodell aus dieser Zeit erhalten.

Die älteste vollständig erhaltene Gesamtkarte Londons wurde 1572 nach einem Stich Frans Hogenbergs angefertigt. Diese Karte zeigt London kurz vor der Regierungszeit von Königin Elizabeth I. zu einer Zeit, als London etwa 75 000 Einwohner zählte.

In der ersten Hälfte des 17. Jahrhunderts entstanden einige Panoramazeichnungen und Ansichten Londons, doch letztlich war es der Große Brand von London (Great Fire) im Jahr 1666, der den nächsten großen Impuls zur Erstellung von Karten, Plänen und Ansichten der Stadt gab. Das Feuer wütete fünf Tage lang auf einer Fläche von etwa 1,5 Quadratkilometern und brannte mehr als 13 000 Häuser und 89 Kirchen nieder, darunter die St. Paul's Cathedral. Achtzig Prozent der City von London wurden zerstört und etwa 80 000 Menschen evakuiert.

Im Zuge des Wiederaufbaus der Stadt wurden die Straßen verbreitert und solide Backsteinhäuser gebaut (vor dem Großen Brand bestanden viele Häuser und öffentliche Gebäude aus leicht brennbarem Holz und Teer). Außerdem entstanden während des mehrjährigen Wiederaufbaus unter der Leitung des Vorsitzenden der Kommission für den Wiederaufbau Londons, Sir Christopher Wren, einige neue Stadtkarten und -pläne.

Im frühen 18. Jahrhundert wurden nur wenige Stadtkarten hergestellt, meist importierte man aus Holland, der Druckermetropole Europas, Neuauflagen oder Neuausgaben alter Karten. Als jedoch im Jahr 1712 eine dreißigprozentige Steuer auf importierte Karten eingeführt wurde, hatte das zur Folge, dass allmählich Londoner Verlage den Druck der Stadtkarten wieder übernahmen. Überdies begann die französische Immigrantenfamilie Rocque einen ehrgeizigen Plan zu verwirklichen: die Vermessung des gesamten Londoner Stadtgebiets. Neun Jahre dauerte es, bis die Karte vollendet war. Sie war in Quadrate unterteilt, mit Referenznummern versehen und beinhaltete auch ein Register aller Straßen. Die Karte wurde 1746 veröffentlicht und bildete die Grundlage zukünftiger Stadtkarten.

Während des 19. Jahrhunderts wurden zuerst in der Zeit von König George I. und dann während der Regency Periode und der Regierungszeit von Königin Victoria nicht nur viele stilvolle Häuser und öffentliche Gebäude errichtet, sondern auch neue Straßen, Kanäle, Straßenbahn- und Eisenbahnlinien angelegt. Dieses sich stetig verändernde Gesicht Londons verlangte aber auch immer wieder nach neuen Karten und Plänen für seine Bürger und die vielen Besucher.

Vorrangig für die 1829 gegründete Stadtpolizei (Metropolitan Police) wurden detaillierte Stadtkarten mit ihren Außenbezirken und später auch mit allen Gemeinden in einem Radius von etwa 25 Kilometern um die Hauptstadt herum angefertigt, dem Gebiet, das später als Greater London oder Großraum London bezeichnet wurde. Die von den städtischen Behörden hergestellten Karten stellen nicht nur ein detailliertes Bild der Abwasser- und Nutzwasserversorgung, der Tunnel und Flüsse Londons dar, es wurden auch Karten hergestellt, die die verschiedenen Bezirke Londons mit ihren unterschiedlichen politischen Tendenzen und der Verteilung des Wohlstands innerhalb der Stadt darstellten.

Das Verkehrswesen war entscheidend für das Wachstum Londons, und so stieg die Nachfrage nach Karten für die öffentlichen Verkehrswege immer mehr. Streckenkarten für den Bahnbetrieb, die dampfbetriebenen Straßenbahnen und die von Pferden gezogenen Busse waren nun unentbehrlich, als diese im viktorianischen London eingeführt wurden – und erneut, als im Jahr 1863 die Electric Railways (heute London Underground oder Tube) eröffnet wurden.

London und dessen Umgebung waren schon immer von großem Interesse für Graveure und Verleger, sie faszinierten Historiker, Illustratoren und Maler, die entweder in der Hauptstadt lebten oder die berühmte Stadt besuchten. Als die Königsfamilie oder andere wohlhabende Familien sich im 16. Jahrhundert Portraits ihrer Verwandten und Bilder ihrer Anwesen anfertigen ließen, kamen Ölgemälde in Mode, die auch bald die Bauwerke Londons und anderer historisch bedeutender Orte zeigten.

Viele Zeichnungen, Stiche und Lithografien zur Geschichte Londons wurden für Bücher, Magazine und Tageszeitungen (wie *Illustrated London News*, *The Times of London* und *Vanity Fair*) hergestellt. Gemälde und Zeichnungen Londons dienten auch dazu, den Status der Stadt als politisches Zentrum Englands mit seiner Finanz- und Handelsmacht zu betonen. Die Themse mit ihren Schiffswerften, Kais, Bargen, Märkten und der Fertigungsindustrie wurde in den Darstellungen zum Symbol der Stärke.

War der Große Brand der Auslöser für die Neugestaltung und das Wachstum des mittelalterlichen London, so war es die Zerstörung während des Zweiten Weltkriegs, die für die heutige Gestalt und Architektur des modernen London verantwortlich ist. Mit dem Ziel, die Finanzindustrie, die Verkehrsbetriebe, die Seewege und den Warenverkehr in und aus der Stadt heraus lahm zu legen, zerstörte die deutsche Luftwaffe zwischen 1940 und 1941 große Teile Londons. Vor allem die Innenstadt wurde zerstört und musste wieder aufgebaut werden. In seinem zeitgenössischen Bild »Lambeth Palace and the House of Commons« zeigt Alfred Daniels das London von heute – mit einer ruhigen Themse und als Stadt, die vorwiegend eine Touristenattraktion ist.

Heutzutage ist die kommerzielle Fotografie die gängigste Technik, um Ansichten einer Stadt festzuhalten. Die meisten modernen Karten Londons dienen als zweckmäßiger Guide, um von einem Teil der Stadt in den anderen zu kommen oder um zu bestimmten Zielen zu gelangen. London-Besucher sind leicht zu erkennen, wenn sie, vertieft in Stadtkarten oder Streckenkarten der U-Bahn, ihren Weg suchen.

INTRODUCTION

La réalisation de cartes géographiques remonte à l'époque de l'Égypte ancienne, et déjà Alexandre le Grand (356–323 avant Jésus-Christ) était accompagné de cartographes au cours de ses conquêtes. Le géographe grec Strabon (né vers 63 avant Jésus-Christ) avait rédigé une *Géographie* se composant de dix-sept volumes, qui contient des informations sur la géographie de l'Europe, l'Asie et l'Afrique. Outre ses propres observations, l'ouvrage comporte également des informations historiques sur les lieux, les hommes et les cultures de cette époque, qu'il avait pu rassembler durant ses voyages.

Bien que les volumes de l'ouvrage existent toujours, la plupart des cartes géographiques n'ont malheureusement pas traversé les siècles, car ce n'est qu'à partir du XVᵉ siècle qu'on s'est penché sur la conservation des cartes géographiques. Alors que la fondation de Londres par les Romains remonte à plus de 2000 ans, les cartes ou les vues de la ville antérieures à 1500 sont peu nombreuses. L'essentiel de la ville s'étendait alors sur un périmètre de 2,5 kilomètres carrés. Une importante partie de la population vivait au-dehors des remparts dans de petites bourgades et des villages.

En raison des changements que subissaient les conditions économiques et la société, des progrès technologiques, de la domination de l'Europe sur les mers et de la colonisation de pays étrangers, Londres grandissait perpétuellement depuis le XVIᵉ siècle au-delà de son enceinte existante. La capitale annexa des villages et des hameaux, les faisant siens comme districts qui, à leur tour, devinrent plus tard les quartiers de Londres. Depuis le centre de la ville, le territoire s'étendait à présent dans un rayon de 25 à 30 kilomètres au-dehors des remparts. Depuis maintenant plus de quatre siècles, les gens se posent toujours la même question, qui s'impose aujourd'hui encore : quelle est la taille de Londres et où s'arrête la ville ?

La réponse à cette question, et à d'autres qui lui sont semblables, est apportée en partie par des cartes. Au début, ce sont surtout des graveurs d'origine hollandaise ou allemande qui utilisaient leurs savoir-faire dans l'art de la gravure et dans la technique de l'impression pour dresser des cartes de Londres. La première carte à l'échelle de Londres connue a vraisemblablement été établie par le cartographe Anthony van den Wyngaerde. Malheureusement, il ne reste plus que des fragments d'une version gravée sur une plaque de cuivre et une maquette en bois de cette époque.

La plus ancienne carte de Londres, entièrement conservée, a été réalisée en 1572 d'après une gravure de Frans Hogenberg. Cette carte montre Londres peu avant le règne de la reine Élisabeth Iʳᵉ, à une époque où Londres comptait environ 75 000 habitants.

Au cours de la première moitié du XVIIᵉ siècle, quelques dessins panoramiques et vues de Londres virent le jour, toutefois, ce fut le Grand Incendie de Londres (Great Fire) en 1666 qui fournit la grande vague d'élan suivante pour établir des cartes, des plans et des vues de la ville. L'incendie, qui avait sévi cinq jours durant sur une superficie d'environ 1,5 kilomètres carrés, avait anéanti plus de 13 000 maisons et 89 églises, parmi lesquelles la cathédrale Saint-Paul. Quatre-vingts pour cent de la cité de Londres furent anéantis, et environ 80 000 personnes évacuées.

Dans le cadre de la reconstruction de la ville qui s'ensuivit, les rues furent agrandies et de solides maisons de briques furent construites (avant le grand incendie, de nombreuses habitations et bâtiments publics étaient en bois et en goudron, facilement inflammables). En outre, au cours des années de reconstruction sous la direction du président de la commission pour la reconstruction de Londres, Sir Christopher Wren, quelques nouvelles cartes et nouveaux plans de la ville virent le jour.

Au début du XVIIIᵉ siècle, seules quelques cartes de la ville furent réalisées, et la plupart du temps, c'est de Hollande, la métropole européenne de l'impression, que l'on importait de nouveaux tirages ou de nouvelles éditions de cartes anciennes. Toutefois, lorsque fut introduit, en 1712, un impôt de trente pour cent sur les cartes importées, des éditeurs londoniens reprirent peu à peu en main l'impression de cartes de leur ville. De plus, la famille française d'immigrants, Rocque, se lança dans un projet ambitieux : l'arpentage de la totalité de la zone urbaine de Londres. Cela prit neuf ans avant que la carte soit finie. Elle était divisée en carrés, munie de numéros de référence, et comprenait également un index de toutes les rues. La carte, parue en 1746, formait la base des futurs plans de la ville.

Durant le XIXᵉ siècle, ce fut tout d'abord sous le règne du roi Georges Iᵉʳ, puis pendant la période Regency et le règne de la reine Victoria, que furent construits non seulement des maisons et des bâtiments publics de style, mais aussi de nouvelles rues, des canaux, des lignes de tram et ferroviaires. Cette physionomie de Londres, sans cesse en proie à des transformations, requérait en permanence de nouvelles cartes et de nouveaux plans pour ses citoyens et ses nombreux visiteurs.

C'est en priorité pour la police municipale (Metropolitan Police), fondée en 1829, que furent dressées des cartes détaillées de la ville, avec leurs agglomérations, et plus tard avec toutes les communes dans un rayon d'environ 25 kilomètres autour de la capitale, ce territoire qui fut plus tard désigné sous le nom de Greater London, ou Grand Londres. Les cartes constituées par l'administration municipale donnaient non seulement une image des canalisations d'eaux usées et industrielles, des tunnels et des fleuves de Londres, mais des cartes représentant les différents districts de Londres avec leurs tendances politiques variées et la répartition de l'aisance au sein de la ville furent aussi dressées.

Le trafic fut un facteur essentiel de la croissance de Londres et la demande de cartes avec les routes publiques augmenta toujours davantage. Lorsqu'ils furent introduits dans le Londres victorien, les plans des correspondances pour le train, les trams à vapeur et les bus hippomobiles étaient à présent devenus indispensables, et le furent à nouveau lors de l'inauguration de l'Electric Railways en 1863 (aujourd'hui le London Underground ou Tube).

Londres et sa région ont toujours intéressé grandement les graveurs et les éditeurs, ils fascinaient les historiens, les illustrateurs et les peintres, qui soit vivaient dans la capitale ou visitaient la célèbre ville. Lorsque, au XVIᵉ siècle, la famille royale ou d'autres familles aisées faisaient exécuter des portraits des membres de leur famille ou des tableaux de leur propriété, les huiles qui représentaient les édifices de Londres et d'autres lieux historiques importants devinrent à la mode.

De nombreux dessins, gravures et lithographies sur l'histoire de Londres ont été réalisés pour des livres, des magazines et des quotidiens (comme *Illustrated London News*, *The Times of London* et *Vanity Fair*). Des tableaux et des dessins de Londres servaient également à souligner le statut de la ville en tant que centre politique de l'Angleterre, avec son pouvoir financier et commercial. La Tamise, avec ses chantiers navals, ses quais, ses barges, ses marchés et son industrie de produits finis, fit office de symbole de la force dans les représentations.

Si le Grand Incendie déclencha le nouvel aménagement et la croissance du Londres médiéval, c'est sa destruction au cours de la Seconde Guerre mondiale qui est responsable des actuels aménagement et architecture du Londres moderne. Avec pour but de paralyser l'industrie de la finance, le trafic, les routes maritimes et le trafic des marchandises dans et hors de la ville, la Luftwaffe endommagea de grandes parties de Londres entre 1940 et 1941, détruisant avant tout le centre ville, qui dut être reconstruit. Le tableau contemporain d'Alfred Daniel, « Lambeth Palace and the House of Common », montre le Londres d'aujourd'hui, avec une Tamise paisible et une ville qui est principalement une attraction touristique.

De nos jours, la photographie commerciale est la technique la plus courante pour fixer une vue de la ville. La plupart des plans modernes de Londres servent de guides adéquats pour parvenir d'un quartier à un autre ou pour traverser la ville vers différentes destinations. Les visiteurs de Londres sont facilement reconnaissables, lorsque, plongés dans leur plan de ville ou leur plan de métro, ils cherchent leur chemin.

CHARLES D'ORLÉANS IN THE TOWER OF LONDON

THE EARLIEST KNOWN PAINTING OF LONDON, C. 1500, ARTIST UNKNOWN

This early-sixteenth-century miniature painting shows an original view of London with the White Tower (now part of the Tower of London), London Bridge, and the City of London (including St. Paul's Cathedral) as they appeared around 1500. This painting, done in England for Henry VII or his son Prince Arthur, in the Flemish style, is considered to be one of the earliest known paintings of London and was painted as the decorative frontispiece to a volume of poems composed by the Duke of Orléans. The Duke, joint commander of the French forces at the Battle of Azincourt, was taken prisoner on the battlefield and held in London for twenty-five years as a hostage.

He is shown in the upper window of the White Tower, where he was kept imprisoned and was released after a ransom of 300,000 crowns was paid; again in the lower gallery, writing to his brother in 1440 to give him news of his pending return; being greeted upon his release; and finally, riding away on horseback through the drawbridge. In the background is the Old London Bridge, and the City of London just beyond.

CHARLES D'ORLÉANS IM TOWER OF LONDON

ÄLTESTES BEKANNTES GEMÄLDE VON LONDON, UM 1500, UNBEKANNTER KÜNSTLER

Diese im frühen 16. Jahrhundert entstandene Miniatur zeigt eine Ansicht Londons mit dem White Tower (heute ein Teil des Tower von London), der London Bridge und dem Zentrum Londons mit der St. Paul's Cathedral, wie sie sich um 1500 darstellte. Das Gemälde, das in England für Henry VII. oder dessen Sohn, Prinz Arthur, im flämischen Stil hergestellt wurde und eines der ältesten bekannten Bilder Londons ist, wurde als dekoratives Frontispiz für einen Gedichtband des Herzogs von Orléans gemalt. Der Herzog, der während der Schlacht von Azincourt Oberbefehlshaber der französischen Streitkräfte war, wurde auf dem Schlachtfeld gefangen genommen und fünfundzwanzig Jahre in London als Geisel festgehalten.

Das Gemälde stellt ihn im oberen Fenster des White Towers dar, wo er inhaftiert und erst gegen ein Lösegeld von 300 000 Kronen freigelassen wurde, sowie rechts in der unteren Galerie, während er im Jahr 1440 in einem Brief an seinen Bruder seine bevorstehende Rückkehr ankündigt. Ferner zeigt das Bild die Begrüßung nach seiner Entlassung und letztlich seinen Ritt über die Zugbrücke gen Heimat.

Im Hintergrund befinden sich die Old London Bridge und die City von London.

CHARLES D'ORLÉANS DANS LA TOUR DE LONDRES

LE PLUS ANCIEN TABLEAU CONNU DE LONDRES, VERS 1500, ARTISTE INCONNU

Cette miniature, qui a vu le jour au début du XVIᵉ siècle, montre une vue de Londres avec la White Tower (une partie de l'actuelle Tour de Londres), le pont de Londres et le centre de la ville avec la cathédrale Saint-Paul, telle qu'elle se présentait vers 1500. L'enluminure, qui fut réalisée en Angleterre dans le style flamand pour Henri VIII ou son fils, le prince Arthur, et qui est l'un des plus anciens tableaux connus de Londres, a été peinte comme frontispice pour décorer un recueil de poèmes du duc d'Orléans. Le duc, qui commandait les troupes françaises durant la bataille d'Azincourt, fut fait prisonnier sur le champ de bataille et retenu en captivité pendant 25 ans à Londres.

Le tableau le représente à la fois se tenant à la fenêtre du haut de la White Tower, où il est détenu, attendant d'être libéré contre une rançon de 300 000 couronnes, ainsi qu'à droite, dans la galerie du bas, tandis qu'en 1440, il rédige une lettre à son frère, lui annonçant son retour imminent. La miniature montre également l'annonce de sa libération et pour finir, la chevauchée de son départ par le pont-levis.

En arrière-plan se devinent le pont Old London Bridge et la cité de Londres.

MAP OF MID-TUDOR LONDON

ENGRAVED BY FRANS HOGENBERG, BASED ON A DRAWING BY GEORGE HOEFNAGEL. PUBLISHED IN *CIVITAS ORBIS TERRARUM* BY BRAUN AND HOGENBERG, 1572

This engraved map is assumed to be the work of Frans Hogenberg and was probably based on a drawing by George Hoefnagel. It shows London in the 1550s just before the reign of Elizabeth I, which began in 1558. London, barely one square mile, is bounded by green fields and the river. At this time, the City of London had a population of about 75,000, with another 150,000 people living outside the medieval walls. The city walls were built on the original Roman foundations. Westminster Abbey is to the west, around the river bend, connected to the city by the main road through Whitehall, Charing Cross, Covent Garden, and across Fleet River. To the east of the city lies the White Tower, now part of the Tower of London. South of the river lies Southwark, a mainly rural area with a small village to the east and the Archbishop of Canterbury's palace at Lambeth Marshes to the west. Old London Bridge is depicted with houses and shops built upon it. It was the only bridge to span the Thames River in London until 1750, when Westminster Bridge was opened.

KARTE LONDONS MITTE DER TUDORZEIT

STICH VON FRANS HOGENBERG, BASIEREND AUF EINER ZEICHNUNG VON GEORG HOEFNAGEL, VERÖFFENTLICHT IN DER *CIVITAS ORBIS TERRARUM* VON BRAUN UND HOGENBERG, 1572

Dieser Stich stammt vermutlich von Frans Hogenberg und basiert möglicherweise auf einer Zeichnung Georg Hoefnagels. Er stellt London um 1550 kurz vor der Regentschaft von Elizabeth I. dar, die 1558 Königin wurde. London war nur knapp 2,5 Quadratkilometer groß, umschlossen vom Fluss und von grünen Wiesen. Zu dieser Zeit zählte London etwa 75 000 Einwohner; weitere 150 000 Menschen lebten außerhalb der mittelalterlichen Mauern, die auf den ursprünglichen römischen Grundmauern errichtet waren. Im Westen, hinter der Flussbiegung, liegt Westminster Abbey, das mit der Stadt über die Hauptstraße durch Whitehall, Charing Cross, Covent Garden und über den Fleet River, einen Nebenfluss der Themse, verbunden ist. Im Osten der Stadt befindet sich der White Tower, der heute zum Tower of London gehört. Südlich des Flusses liegt Southwark, ein hauptsächlich ländliches Gebiet mit einem kleinen Dorf im Osten und dem Palast des Erzbischofs von Canterbury in Lambeth Marshes im Westen. Die Old London Bridge ist mit auf ihr gebauten Wohnhäusern und Geschäften abgebildet. Bis zur Fertigstellung der Westminster Bridge 1750 war dies die einzige Brücke über die Themse.

CARTE DE LONDRES DU MILIEU DE L'ÉPOQUE TUDOR

GRAVURE DE FRANS HOGENBERG, BASÉE SUR UN DESSIN DE GEORGES HOEFNAGEL, PUBLIÉE DANS *CIVITAS ORBIS TERRARUM* DE BRAUN ET HOGENBERG, 1572

Vraisemblablement due à Frans Hogenberg, cette gravure a probablement vu le jour sur la base d'un dessin de Hoefnagel. Londres y est représenté vers 1550, peu avant la régence d'Élisabeth Iʳᵉ, devenue reine en 1558. La ville n'atteignait alors qu'une superficie de 2,5 kilomètres carrés, bordée du fleuve et de vertes prairies, et comptait environ 75 000 habitants à cette époque ; 150 000 autres personnes vivaient au-dehors de l'enceinte médiévale, qui avait été érigée sur les murs de fondation romains. À l'ouest, derrière le coude du fleuve, se situe l'abbaye de Westminster, qui était reliée à la ville par la route principale, traversant Whitehall, Charing Cross, Covent Garden et franchissait Fleet River, un bras de la Tamise. À l'est de la ville se trouve la tour Blanche, qui fait aujourd'hui partie de la Tour de Londres. Au sud du fleuve est situé Southwark, une région principalement rurale, avec un petit village à l'est et le palais Lambeth de l'archevêque de Canterbury, dans le marais de Lambeth Marsh, à l'ouest. Le pont Old London Bridge, avec ses maisons et ses boutiques, est aussi reproduit. Jusqu'à ce que le pont de Westminster ait été achevé en 1750, c'était l'unique pont enjambant la Tamise.

A Frost Fair on the Thames at Temple Stairs

Oil on canvas by Abraham Hondius, c. 1684

Due to the narrow arches and breakwaters of the Old London Bridge, the Thames River froze over on a number of occasions and paralyzed river traffic. In 1684, the cold weather froze the river upstream from the bridge and street fairs were created by building tents on the ice between Temple Stairs and the South Bank. Various sporting events were held, including bull baiting, bear baiting, and fox hunting, as well as games and activities such as dancing, ox roasting, football, ninepins, and horse sledding. The horses' hooves were either spiked or wrapped in linen cloth to give them a grip on the ice. Even King Charles II and the royal family visited the Frost Fair. The view depicts the king's visit, which was celebrated with the firing of three cannons by the Household Cavalry. The freeze lasted from mid-December to mid-February.

Records reveal that the Thames froze twenty-three times beginning in 1309, and Frost Fairs were recorded in 1677, 1684, 1715, 1739, 1789 and 1814. The last Frost Fair was held in 1831, before the New London Bridge was opened.

Frostjahrmarkt auf der Themse bei Temple Stairs

Öl auf Leinwand von Abraham Hondius, um 1684

Aufgrund der schmalen Bögen und der Wasserbrecher der Old London Bridge fror die Themse einige Male zu und brachte so den Schiffsverkehr komplett zum Erliegen. Im Jahr 1684 fror die Themse flussaufwärts der Brücke vollständig zu, und auf dem Eis zwischen der Straße Temple Stairs und dem Südufer baute man Zelte, und ein kleiner Jahrmarkt entstand. Mannigfaltige Sportveranstaltungen wie Bullenbeißen (bull baiting), Bärenhetze (bear baiting) und Fuchsjagd fanden statt, zudem auch Spiele und Attraktionen wie Tanzveranstaltungen, Ochsenbraten, Fußball, Kegeln und Pferdeschlittenfahrten. Die Hufe der Pferde wurden entweder mit Nägeln oder Eisenspitzen versehen oder in Leinentücher gewickelt, damit sie auf dem Eis griffen. Sogar König Charles II. und die königliche Familie besuchten den Frostjahrmarkt. Das Gemälde zeigt den Besuch des Königs, der mit dem Abfeuern von drei Kanonen durch die Gardekavallerie (Household Cavalry) gefeiert wird. Der Frost dauerte von Mitte Dezember bis Mitte Februar.

Aufzeichnungen belegen, dass die Themse seit 1309 dreiundzwanzig Mal zufror; die Frostjahrmärkte fanden in den Jahren 1677, 1684, 1715, 1739, 1789 und 1814. Der letzte Frostmarkt fand im Jahr 1831 statt, bevor die New London Bridge eröffnet wurde.

Foire du gel sur la Tamise près de Temple Stairs

Huile sur toile d'Abraham Hondius, vers 1684

À cause des arches étroites et des brise-vagues du Old London Bridge, la Tamise gela plusieurs fois, paralysant ainsi tout le trafic fluvial. En 1684, la Tamise fut totalement prise dans les glaces en amont du pont, et entre la rue de Temple Stairs et la rive sud, des tentes furent érigées et une petite foire vit le jour sur la glace. Diverses manifestations comme le combat de taureaux et de chiens (bull baiting), d'ours et de chiens (bear baiting) et la chasse au renard avaient lieu, de même que des jeux et des attractions comme des bals, du bœuf à la broche, football, de quilles et des sorties en traîneaux à cheval. Les sabots des chevaux étaient soit munis de clous ou de pointes de fer, soit enveloppés dans des chiffons de lin afin qu'ils accrochent sur la glace. Même le roi Charles II et la famille royale rendirent visite à la frost fair. Le tableau montre la visite du roi, qui est saluée la mise à feu de trois canons par la cavalerie montée (Household Cavalry).

Le gel se prolongea de la mi-décembre à la mi-février. Des récits témoignent que, depuis 1309, la Tamise gela vingt-trois fois ; les frost fairs se sont tenues en 1677, 1684, 1715, 1739, 1789 et 1814. La dernière frost fair a eu lieu en 1831, avant que le New London Bridge soit ouvert.

THE GREAT FIRE OF LONDON 1666

OIL ON WOOD, DUTCH SCHOOL,
C. 1666, ARTIST UNKNOWN

The Great Fire of London broke out in the early morning of September 2, 1666, on Pudding Lane in a bakeshop that catered to Charles II. The city was just recovering from yet another plague, and the dead were still being buried in mass graves.
The fire, fanned by winds and kindled by pitch-coated wooden buildings, burned westward and across London Bridge and consumed 80 percent of the City of London (some 430 acres), destroying 13,000 houses, 89 churches, including St. Paul's Cathedral and the Guildhall. Remarkably, only ten known deaths were recorded as a result of the fire, which raged for nearly five days. Almost eighty thousand people were evacuated (the total population at that time was four hundred thousand) and some twenty thousand choose not to return to the city. Plague, however, was eradicated due to the mass death of rats. Fire insurance became popular.
The view shows St. Paul's Cathedral in the center of the fire and Old London Bridge to the left. The Tower of London is shown clearly to the right of the painting.

DER GROSSE BRAND VON LONDON 1666

ÖL AUF HOLZ, NIEDERLÄNDISCHE SCHULE,
UM 1666, KÜNSTLER UNBEKANNT

In den frühen Morgenstunden des 2. September 1666 brach der Große Brand von London (Great Fire) in der königlichen Bäckerei, die Charles II. versorgte, an der Pudding Lane aus. Die Stadt erholte sich gerade von einer anderen Katastrophe, der Pest – noch immer fanden Bestattungen der Opfer statt.
Das Feuer, angefacht durch Wind und durch die mit Pech beschichteten Holzhäuser, fraß sich gen Westen und über die London Bridge und zerstörte fast achtzig Prozent der City von London. Auf etwa 1,5 Quadratkilometern fielen schätzungsweise 13 000 Häuser und 89 Kirchen, darunter die St. Paul's Cathedral und auch die Guildhall, dem Feuer zum Opfer.
Bemerkenswert ist, dass das während fünf Tagen wütende Feuer nur zehn Todesopfer forderte, allerdings wurden nahezu achtzigtausend Menschen evakuiert und etwa zwanzigtausend Menschen kehrten London für immer den Rücken (die Gesamteinwohnerzahl belief sich zu dieser Zeit auf ungefähr vierhunderttausend). Durch die mit dem Feuer verbundene Ausrottung der Ratten wurde allerdings eine weitere Ausbreitung der Pest verhindert. Feuerversicherungen kamen in Mode.
Die Ansicht zeigt die St. Paul's Cathedral im Zentrum des Feuers und links die Old London Bridge. Im rechten Teil des Gemäldes ist der Tower von London abgebildet.

LE GRAND INCENDIE DE LONDRES EN 1666

HUILE SUR BOIS, ÉCOLE HOLLANDAISE,
VERS 1666, ARTISTE INCONNU

Au cours des premières heures du 2 septembre 1666 se déclencha le Grand Incendie de Londres (Great Fire), dans la boulangerie royale de Pudding Lane, qui approvisionnait Charles II. La ville était juste en train de se relever d'une autre catastrophe : la peste, et les inhumations des victimes n'étaient même pas terminées.
Le feu, attisé par le vent et alimenté par les maisons en bois recouvertes de goudron, se propagea en direction de l'ouest et par le pont de Londres, détruisant ainsi presque quatre-vingts pour cent de la City de Londres. Sur environ 1,5 kilomètres carrés, on estime que 13 000 habitations et 89 églises, parmi lesquelles la cathédrale Saint-Paul, ainsi que Guildhall, ont été la proie des flammes.
Ce qui est remarquable, c'est que pendant les cinq jours durant lesquels sévit le feu, seules dix victimes furent à déplorer. Cependant, il faut évoquer que presque quatre-vingt mille personnes furent évacuées et qu'environ vingt mille tournèrent définitivement le dos à Londres (le nombre total d'habitants se montait à l'époque à environ quatre cent mille). L'extermination des rats par le feu eut toutefois pour effet d'empêcher une nouvelle propagation de la peste. Des assurances incendie devinrent à la mode.
La vue montre la cathédrale Saint-Paul au centre du feu, et à gauche, le pont Old London Bridge. Dans la partie droite du tableau est représentée la Tour de Londres.

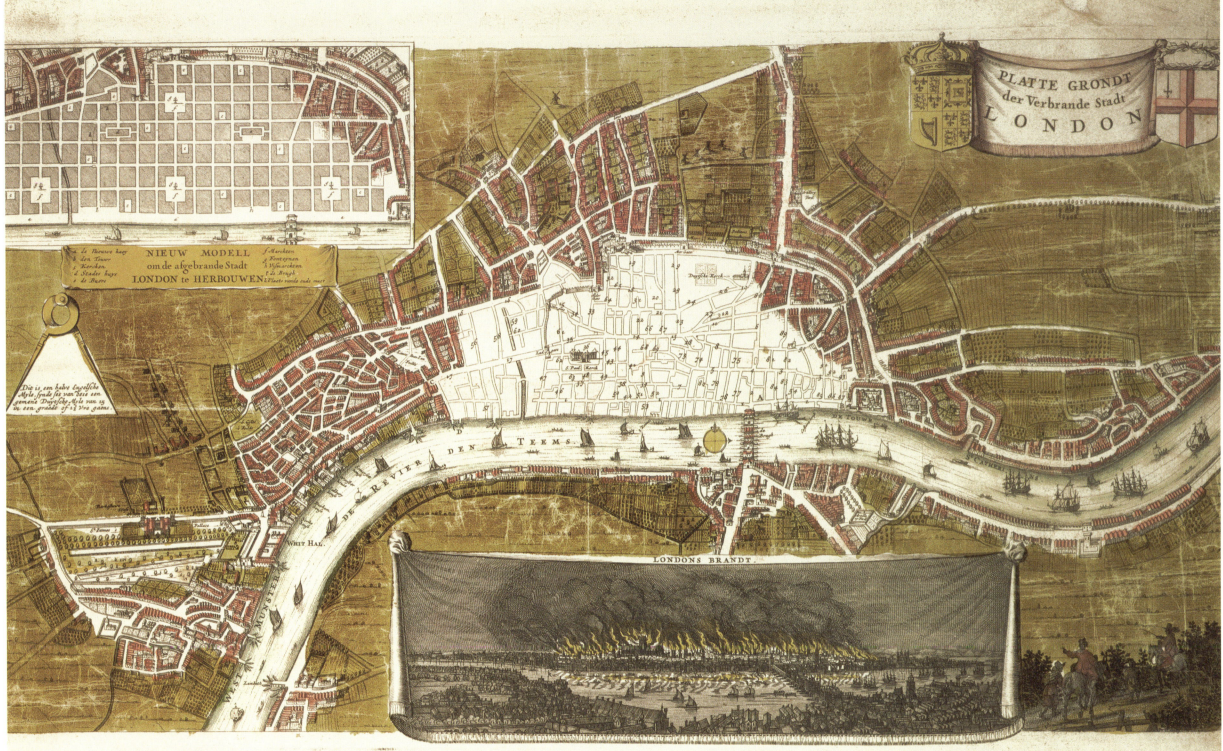

Afbeelding van de	Representation curieuse de l'embrasement de la	Delineation of the
STADT LONDON.	**VILLE de LONDRES,**	**CITIE LONDON,**
Aenwijzende hoe verre de zelve verbrandt is, en wat plaetzen noch overgebleven zijn.	Avec une Demonstration exacte de ce qui en est demuré de reste.	Shewing how far the said citie is burnt down, and what places doe yet remain standing.

After the Great Fire of London

COLORED ENGRAVING BY MARCUS WILLEMSZ
DOORNIK DEPICTING THE FIRE,
THE AREA DESTROYED BY THE FIRE,
AND THE PROPOSED PLANS FOR REBUILDING
THE CITY, C. 1675

After the Great Fire of London in 1666, a plan was drawn up to provide the city with wider streets and brick buildings. Sir Christopher Wren was commissioned to design and supervise the construction of fifty-one new churches, including the reconstruction of St. Paul's Cathedral, which was destroyed in the fire. In 1676, another fire south of the Thames River destroyed six hundred houses. These two fires created an opportunity to radically remake the city and changed the face of London forever. The six commissioners appointed to redesign the city drew up the most comprehensive town-planning legislation ever seen in England.

Rebuilding continued in spite of the wars with the Dutch, the Monmouth Rebellion, and the revolution of 1688. By 1671, nine thousand brick buildings had been erected. St. Paul's Cathedral was rebuilt between 1675 and 1710 and was considered the crowning glory of Wren's remarkable body of work.

Many of the residents who fled the fires did not return to the city.

Nach dem Grossen Brand von London

KOLORIERTER STICH VON MARCUS WILLEMSZ
DOORNIK, DARSTELLUNG DES VOM FEUER
ZERSTÖRTEN GEBIETS UND DIE
VORGESCHLAGENEN PLÄNE FÜR DEN
WIEDERAUFBAU DER STADT, UM 1675

Nach dem Großen Brand im Jahr 1666 wurde ein Plan entworfen, nach dem London durch den Bau von breiteren Straßen und soliden Backsteinbauten profitieren sollte. Sir Christopher Wren wurde mit der Planung und der Bauaufsicht für 51 neue Kirchen beauftragt, darunter auch der Wiederaufbau der vom Feuer zerstörten St. Paul's Cathedral. 1676 zerstörte allerdings erneut ein Feuer auf der Südseite der Themse an die 600 Häuser. Die beiden Großbrände eröffneten den Planern die Möglichkeit, die Stadt grundlegend neu zu gestalten, und so veränderten sie das Gesicht Londons für immer. Sechs Kommissionsmitglieder waren mit der Neugestaltung der Stadt betraut und verfassten die umfangreichsten Stadtplanungsvorschriften, die jemals in England erstellt wurden.

Auch während der Kriege gegen Holland, der Monmouth Rebellion und der Revolution 1688 setzte sich der Wiederaufbau fort, der bis 1671 9000 neue Backsteingebäude entstehen ließ. Der Aufbau der St. Paul's Cathedral dauerte von 1675 bis 1710 und wird als der krönende Abschluss der bemerkenswerten Arbeit Wrens angesehen.

Viele der während der Feuersbrunst geflohenen Einwohner Londons kehrten nie wieder in die Stadt zurück.

Après le Grand Incendie de Londres

GRAVURE COLORIÉE DE MARCUS WILLEMSZ
DOORNIK, REPRÉSENTATION DU PÉRIMÈTRE
DÉTRUIT PAR LES FLAMMES ET DES PLANS
SUGGÉRÉS POUR RECONSTRUIRE LA VILLE,
VERS 1675

Après le Grand Incendie en 1666, un plan fut conçu, selon lequel Londres devait profiter de la construction de rues plus larges et de bâtiments solides en brique. Sir Christopher Wren fut chargé de la planification et du contrôle des chantiers de 51 nouvelles églises, parmi lesquelles la cathédrale Saint-Paul, qui avait, elle aussi, été détruite par le feu. Toutefois, en 1676, un nouvel incendie détruisit près de 600 maisons sur le côté sud de la Tamise. Les deux grands incendies donnaient aux urbanistes la possibilité de réaménager la ville de fond en comble, et ils changèrent donc la physionomie de Londres à tout jamais. Six membres de la commission étaient chargés du réaménagement de la ville et rédigèrent les directives d'urbanisation les plus détaillées qui furent jamais établies en Angleterre.

Également durant la guerre contre la Hollande, puis pendant la rébellion dite de « Monmouth » et la révolution de 1688, la reconstruction continua, faisant voir le jour à 9000 nouveaux bâtiments de briques jusqu'en 1671. La construction de la cathédrale Saint-Paul dura de 1675 à 1710, et elle est considérée comme l'apogée du travail remarquable de Wren.

Nombre d'habitants qui avaient fui l'enfer du feu ne retournèrent jamais à Londres.

LONDON FROM SOUTHWARK

OIL ON WOOD, C. 1630, ARTIST UNKNOWN

This view shows London as seen from the south side of the Thames River as it appeared in 1630, before the Great Fire of London. In the foreground are the playhouses (the Globe Theatre, the Rose Theatre, the Hope Theatre and the Swan Theatre) and the Church of St. Mary Overy (later to become Southwark Cathedral).
The wooden London Bridge is overcrowded with houses and shops and Thomas à Becket Chapel. In the center of the bridge is a drawbridge, which would have allowed tall sailing ships and galleons to pass through. Also on the bridge is Nonsuch House, thought to be the residence of the lord mayor of London.
Note the heads of executed convicts on poles atop the building at the southern end of the bridge. They were left there to deter the population from criminal acts.
St. Paul's Cathedral dominates the city, much of which was to be subsequently destroyed by the Great Fire. The Tower of London is shown to the right of the panoramic view.

BLICK AUF LONDON VON SOUTHWARK AUS

ÖL AUF HOLZ, UM 1630, UNBEKANNTER KÜNSTLER

Dieses Gemälde zeigt London von der Südseite der Themse aus, so wie es sich dem Künstler um 1630 vor dem Großen Brand präsentierte. Im Vordergrund befinden sich die verschiedenen Theatergebäude (Globe Theatre, Rose Theatre, Hope Theatre und Swan Theatre) und die St. Mary Overy Kirche, die später in Southwark Cathedral umbenannt wurde.
Auf der hölzernen London Bridge sieht man Wohnhäuser und Geschäfte dicht aneinander gedrängt sowie die Thomas à Becket Chapel und das Nonsuch House, von dem angenommen wird, dass es das Wohnhaus des Oberbürgermeisters von London war. In der Mitte der Brücke befindet sich eine Zugbrücke, die großen Segelschiffen und Galeonen die Durchfahrt ermöglichte. Bemerkenswert sind auch die auf Holzstangen aufgespießten Köpfe von hingerichteten Sträflingen am Südende der Brücke, die der Abschreckung der Bevölkerung vor Straftaten dienen sollten.
Die St. Paul's Cathedral, die später beim Großen Brand von London völlig zerstört wurde, dominiert das Stadtbild. Der Tower von London befindet sich auf der rechten Seite dieser Ansicht.

VUE DE LONDRES DEPUIS SOUTHWARK

HUILE SUR BOIS, VERS 1630, AUTEUR INCONNU

Ce tableau montre Londres depuis le côté sud de la Tamise, tel qu'il se présentait à l'artiste aux alentours de 1630 avant le Grand Incendie. Au premier plan se trouvent les différents théâtres (Globe Theatre, Rose Theatre, Hope Theatre et Swan Theatre) et l'église St. Mary-Overy, qui fut plus tard rebaptisée cathédrale de Southwark.
Sur le pont de Londres en bois, on voit des habitations et des boutiques, serrées les unes contre les autres, ainsi que la chapelle Thomas à Becket et la Nonsuch House, dont on suppose que c'était la demeure du bourgmestre principal de Londres. Le milieu du pont est aménagé en pont-levis, pour permettre le passage des grands voiliers et des galions. À noter sont également les têtes de condamnés exécutés, empalées sur des perches en bois à l'extrémité sud du pont, et destinées à dissuader la population de commettre des délits.
La cathédrale Saint-Paul, qui fut entièrement détruite par le Grand Incendie de Londres, domine l'image de la ville. La Tour de Londres est sur la droite de cette vue.

A PROSPECT of the CITY of LONDON.

PANORAMIC VIEW OF LONDON

COPPER ENGRAVING BY MARTIN ENGELBRECHT, C. 1750

This panorama of churches represents many of those that were rebuilt by Sir Christopher Wren, or under his supervision, after the Great Fire of London in 1666, which destroyed or badly damaged eighty-nine churches, including St. Paul's Cathedral. As the head of the Commission for the Rebuildings, Wren was responsible for rebuilding many of those churches, the best known of which were St. Stephen at Walbrook, St. Mary on Abchurch Lane, St. Bride on Fleet Street, St. Mary-le-Bow, and of course, St. Paul's.

In the fifty-seven years between the Great Fire and his death, Wren's rate of rebuilding was astonishing; he established his own style of architecture, which greatly influenced other architects. He was also responsible for the design of the Custom House and Royal Hospital Chelsea.

PANORAMA VON LONDON

KUPFERSTICH VON MARTIN ENGELBRECHT, UM 1750

Dieser Panoramablick zeigt viele der von Sir Christopher Wren selbst oder unter dessen Aufsicht wieder aufgebauten Kirchen nach dem Großen Brand von London im Jahr 1666, bei dem 89 Kirchen zerstört oder schwer beschädigt wurden, darunter auch die St. Paul's Cathedral. Als Vorsitzender der Wiederaufbaukommission war Wren verantwortlich für den Wiederaufbau vieler dieser Kirchen, die bekanntesten darunter sind St. Stephen an der Walbrook, St. Mary an der Abchurch Lane, St. Bride an der Fleet Street, St. Mary-le-Bow und natürlich St. Paul's. Außerdem betreute Wren die Gestaltung des Zollgebäudes und des Royal Hospital Chelsea.

In den siebenundfünfzig Jahren zwischen dem Großen Brand und Wrens Tod war die Geschwindigkeit, mit der er den Wiederaufbau Londons vorantrieb, erstaunlich; zudem beeinflusste sein Architekturstil auch andere Architekten nachhaltig.

PANORAMA DE LONDRES

GRAVURE SUR CUIVRE DE MARTIN ENGELBRECHT, VERS 1750

Cette vue panoramique montre de nombreuses églises, reconstruites soit par les soins de Sir Christopher Wren, soit sous sa surveillance, après le Grand Incendie de Londres de 1666, au cours duquel 89 églises furent détruites ou sévèrement endommagées et parmi lesquelles se trouvait la cathédrale Saint-Paul. En tant que président de la commission de reconstruction, Wren était responsable de la reconstruction de ces nombreuses églises, les plus connues parmi elles étant St. Stephen Walbrook, St. Mary dans la Abchurch Lane, St. Bride dans la Fleet Street, St. Mary-le-Bow et bien sûr, Saint-Paul. De plus, Wren s'occupa de l'aménagement du bâtiment des douanes et du Royal Hospital Chelsea.

Durant les cinquante-sept années qui séparèrent le Grand Incendie de la mort de Wren, la rapidité à laquelle il fit avancer la reconstruction de Londres est étonnante ; de surcroît, son style architectural exerça une influence durable sur d'autres architectes.

THE TOWER OF LONDON

ENGRAVING BY CHARLES RIVIÈRE IN THE STYLE OF ACHILLE LOUIS MARTINET, C. 1862

After defeating King Harold II in the Battle of Hastings (the Saxon king was mortally wounded when an arrow struck his eye), the Normandy invader, William the Conqueror, was hastily crowned king at Westminster Abbey. He soon thereafter began construction on the Tower of London, starting with the White Tower in 1078. The Tower of London was designed to accommodate the king, the royal family, its household, and the king's treasure. The inner defense walls, made up of twelve towers, were added later by King Henry III (1216–1272). King Edward I (1272–1307) added the outer defenses, including the Traitor's Gate (used to transport criminals who had committed or plotted treason against the king from the Thames River to the Tower of London). The Tower became the place of imprisonment, torture, and execution. After his brother King Edward IV died suddenly and unexpectedly in 1483, it is reputed that Richard III had his nephew and younger brother murdered in the tower as he was preparing for his own coronation. Elizabeth I ordered the execution of her cousin Mary Stuart at the tower in 1587. Mary had been imprisoned in the tower for years after she was linked to an assassination attempt on Queen Elizabeth in St. James's Park.

DER TOWER VON LONDON

STICH VON CHARLES RIVIÈRE IM STIL VON ACHILLE LOUIS MARTINET, UM 1862

Nach dem Sieg über König Harold II. in der Schlacht bei Hastings, bei der der angelsächsische König durch einen Pfeil tödlich getroffen wurde, ließ sich der normannische Angreifer, Wilhelm der Eroberer, in der Westminster Abbey eiligst zum neuen König Wilhelm I. krönen. Bald danach begannen im Jahr 1078 die Arbeiten am White Tower, der später Teil des Towers von London werden sollte und so konzipiert wurde, dass er dem König, der königlichen Familie, deren Personal und dem Kronschatz Platz bieten sollte. Die inneren Wehrmauern aus zwölf Türmen wurden später von König Henry III. (1216–1272) hinzugefügt. König Edward I. (1272–1307) ließ die Außenschutze hinzufügen, darunter das Verrätertor, das eigens dazu diente, Verbrecher, die Hochverrat gegen die Krone begangen hatten oder geplant hatten, von der Themse aus in den Tower von London zu bringen. Der Tower wurde ein Ort des Freiheitsentzugs, ein Ort der Folter und der Hinrichtungen. Es wird gemutmaßt, dass Richard III. 1483 nach dem plötzlichen und unerwarteten Tod seines Bruders König Edward IV. seinen Neffen und seinen jüngeren Bruder im Tower hat umbringen gelassen, während er sich auf seine Krönung vorbereitete. 1587 gab Elizabeth I. im Tower den Befehl zur Hinrichtung ihrer Kusine Mary Stuart, die bereits lange Jahre im Tower eingesperrt war, nachdem sie mit einem Attentatsversuch auf Königin Elizabeth im St. James's Park in Verbindung gebracht worden war.

LA TOUR DE LONDRES

GRAVURE DE CHARLES RIVIÈRE DANS LE STYLE D'ACHILLE LOUIS MARTINET, VERS 1862

Après la victoire sur le roi Harold II pendant la bataille de Hastings, au cours de laquelle le roi anglo-saxon fut atteint par une flèche mortelle, l'envahisseur normand, Guillaume le Conquérant, se hâta de se faire couronner à Westminster Abbey, sous le nom de Guillaume Ier. Peu après, en 1078, commencèrent les travaux de la tour Blanche, qui devait devenir plus tard une partie de la Tour de Londres, et qui fut conçue pour abriter le roi, la famille royale, ses domestiques et les joyaux de la couronne. Les remparts intérieurs, flanqués de douze tournelles, furent ajoutés plus tard par le roi Henri III (1216–1272). Le roi Édouard Ier (1272–1307) fit rajouter les défenses extérieures, parmi lesquelles la porte des Traîtres, qui servait spécialement à faire pénétrer dans la Tour de Londres, depuis la Tamise, les criminels qui avaient trahi ou comploté contre la couronne.
La Tour devint un lieu d'enfermement, de torture et d'exécution. On suppose qu'en 1483, Richard III, après la mort soudaine et inattendue de son frère, le roi Édouard IV, a fait assassiner son neveu et son plus jeune frère dans la Tour, tandis qu'il se préparait à être couronné. En 1587, Élisabeth Ire donna l'ordre d'exécuter sa cousine Marie Stuart, reine d'Écosse, qui était déjà enfermée depuis de longues années dans la Tour, après que sa complicité dans une tentative d'attentat contre la reine Élisabeth à St. James's Park fut établie.

FAIRBURNS MAP OF THE COUNTRY TWELVE MILES ROUND LONDON

CHART AND MAP ENGRAVED BY E. BOURNE,
PUBLISHED BY JOHN FAIRBURN,
AUGUST 1, 1798

Many of the major roads leading out of London were established by the Roman army connecting Londinium – as the city was known when first settled by the invaders in AD 60 – with other major garrisons, such as Verulamium (now St. Albans), Camulodunum (now Colchester), Durovernum (now Canterbury), and Aquae Sulis (now Bath – the site of the Roman spa baths).
During the Roman occupation of London, many of the Saxons lived outside the city and established villages where farming was the primary occupation.
By the eighteenth century the area around London had grown to a large metropolis of towns and villages that made up the counties of Kent, Essex, Middlesex, Surrey, and London. Travel was by foot, horse, or horse-drawn carriage, and therefore many coaching inns were established along the main roads leading in and out of London.
The view on the bottom left shows Chelsea Hospital, and the view on the right is of Greenwich Hospital.

FAIRBURNS KARTE VON LONDON IM UMKREIS VON ETWA DREISSIG KILOMETERN

ZEICHNUNG UND KARTE VON E. BOURNE,
HERAUSGEGEBEN VON JOHN FAIRBURN,
1. AUGUST 1798

Die meisten der aus London führenden Straßen wurden von der römischen Armee angelegt, um Londinium, wie die Besatzer 60 n. Chr. die Siedlung nannten, mit anderen wichtigen Garnisonsstützpunkten zu verbinden, so etwa Verulamium (heute St. Albans), Camulodunum (heute Colchester), Durovernum Cantiacorum (heute Canterbury) und Aquae Sulis (heute Bath – bekannt für seine römischen Bäder).
Während der römischen Besatzung Londons lebten viele Angelsachsen außerhalb der Stadt und gründeten dort kleine Bauerndörfer.
Bis zum 18. Jahrhundert hatte sich das Gebiet um London zu einem Ballungsraum mit vielen kleinen Städten und Dörfern entwickelt, die die Grafschaften Kent, Essex, Middlesex, Surrey und London umfassten. Etliche Herbergen entstanden entlang der Hauptstraßen von und nach London und boten Reisenden zu Fuß, zu Pferd oder per Kutsche Rastmöglichkeiten und Obdach.
Die Ansicht im unteren Teil zeigt links das Chelsea Hospital und rechts das Greenwich Hospital.

CARTE DE LONDRES ET DE SES ENVIRONS SUR UNE TRENTAINE DE KILOMÈTRES, PAR FAIRBURN

DESSIN ET CARTE DE E. BOURNE,
PUBLIÉS PAR JOHN FAIRBURN,
1ER AOÛT 1798

La plupart des routes menant hors de Londres ont été tracées par l'armée romaine afin de relier Londinium, ainsi que les occupants nommaient leur colonie en 60 après Jésus-Christ, avec d'autres garnisons importantes, telles que, par exemple, Verulamium (aujourd'hui St. Albans), Camulodunum (Colchester), Durovernum Cantiacorum (Canterbury) et Aquae Sulis (Bath, connue pour ses thermes romains).
Au cours de l'occupation romaine de Londres, de nombreux Anglo-Saxons vivaient en dehors de la ville et fondèrent de petits villages.
Jusqu'au XVIIIe siècle, la région autour de Londres s'était développée en conurbation avec énormément de petites villes et de villages, comprenant les duchés de Kent, Essex, Middlesex, Surrey et Londres. De multiples auberges virent le jour le long des routes principales vers Londres, offrant aux voyageurs à pied, à cheval ou en diligence un relais et un toit.
La vue, dans sa partie inférieure, montre à gauche Chelsea Hospital, et à droite, Greenwich Hospital.

London's Docklands at Wapping, Late Eighteenth Century

Engraving by Thomas & William Daniell, 1803

England's navy was built under the direction of Elizabeth I, when she became Queen in 1558, as a strong wall and defense against the enemies of England, who at the time consisted mainly of Spain. The rise of the navy led to the establishment of the Royal Dockyards in Deptford and Woolwich, and the many private dockyards that lined the Thames River from the Medway to London Bridge, including the Limehouse and Wapping dockyards. It was during this early period that Sir Francis Drake first sailed around the world in a journey lasting some three years and four months, ending in London in 1581.

It was, however, the merchant or commercial shipping that ushered in the vast network of docklands. For 250 years, commencing with regulations dating from the time of Elizabeth I, every ship coming up the Thames River had to unload all dutiable cargo at the twenty quays, known as the Legal Quays, that were crowded side by side between London Bridge and the Tower of London at Wapping. Legal Quays included the London Docks, built at the beginning of the nineteenth century, and St. Katharine Docks, which was added in 1828.

Londoner Hafenviertel bei Wapping, spätes 18. Jahrhundert

Kupferstich von Thomas & William Daniell, 1803

Nachdem Elizabeth I. 1558 zur Königin gekrönt wurde, baute sie zur Verteidigung gegen die Feinde Englands, damals vor allem die Spanier, England zu einer führenden Seemacht auf. Der Ausbau der Marine hatte den Bau königlicher Werften in Deptford und Woolwich sowie die Gründung vieler privater Werften zur Folge, so etwa die Werften in Limehouse und Wapping, die sich entlang der Themse von Medway zur London Bridge befinden. Zu dieser Zeit reiste auch Sir Francis Drake um die Welt – eine Reise, die drei Jahre und vier Monate dauern sollte und erst im Jahr 1581 in London endete.

Doch war es letztlich die Handels- und Güterschifffahrt, die zum Ausbau des weit verzweigten Hafenviertels führte. 250 Jahre lang musste jedes auf der Themse flussaufwärts fahrende Schiff seine gesamte zollpflichtige Ladung an einem der zwanzig Kais, bekannt unter dem Namen Legal Quays (Freihafen), entladen, die sich dicht gedrängt zwischen der London Bridge und dem Tower von London bei Wapping befanden. Dies ging aus einer Vorschrift aus der Zeit von Königin Elizabeth I. hervor. Zu den Legal Quays gehörten später auch die London Docks, die Anfang des 19. Jahrhunderts gebaut wurden, sowie die 1828 hinzu gekommenen St. Katharine Docks.

Le quartier du port de Londres près de Wapping, fin du XVIIIe siècle

Gravure sur cuivre de Thomas & William Daniell, 1803

Pour défendre l'Angleterre contre ses ennemis qui, à l'époque, étaient avant tout les Espagnols, Élisabeth Ire, après son couronnement en 1558, fit de la marine anglaise l'instrument de la puissance maritime du pays. La constitution de la flotte eut pour conséquence la construction de chantiers navals royaux à Deptford et Woolwich, ainsi que la création de nombreux chantiers navals privés, comme, par exemple, les chantiers à Limehouse et à Wapping, qui se trouvaient le long de la Tamise de Medway jusqu'au London Bridge. C'est à cette époque que Sir Francis Drake effectua un tour du monde, un voyage qui devait durer trois ans et quatre mois, pour s'achever en 1581 à Londres.

Toutefois, ce fut pour finir la marine marchande qui mena à l'agrandissement du quartier portuaire, largement ramifié. Pendant 250 ans, chaque navire remontant la Tamise devait décharger la totalité de sa cargaison, soumise aux droits de douane, sur l'un des vingt quais, connus sous le nom de Legal Quays (port franc), qui se serraient entre le London Bridge et la Tour de Londres près de Wapping. Ceci remontait à un règlement de l'époque de la reine Élisabeth Ire. Pus tard, les docks londoniens, qui furent construits au début du XIXe siècle, firent également partie des Legal Quays, ainsi que les St. Katharine Docks qui y furent ajoutés en 1828.

The Road from London West to the City of Bristol

Map by John Ogilby, 1675

John Ogilby was His Majesty's (Charles II) cartographer and was responsible for a number of the maps of the City of London. He also created the first encyclopedia of maps of England.

The road to Bristol was first established by Roman soldiers for their movements and to ferry supplies. The Romans were practical road engineers and therefore built roads that were raised and cambered so the rain would run off. The road was essential because it connected the City of London not only to the spas in Bath, but also to the seaport of Bristol for access to Wales and Ireland.

Die Strasse vom Londoner Westen nach Bristol

Karte von John Ogilby, 1675

John Ogilby war Kartograf des Königs Charles II. und für eine Vielzahl von Karten der Stadt London verantwortlich. Außerdem erstellte er die erste Kartenenzyklopädie Englands.

Die Straße nach Bristol, die London nicht nur mit den Bädern in Bath, sondern auch mit der Hafenstadt Bristol und so mit Wales und Irland verband, wurde von den römischen Besatzern als Transportweg für Truppen und Nachschub geschaffen. Die Römer waren erfahrene Straßenbauer und legten daher diese wichtige Straße höher und gewölbt an, so dass der Regen abfließen konnte.

Les routes de l'ouest de Londres vers Bristol

Carte de John Ogilby, 1675

John Ogilby était le cartographe du roi Charles II et responsable d'un grand nombre de cartes de la ville de Londres. Il a en outre établi le premier atlas d'Angleterre . La route vers Bristol, qui reliait Londres non seulement aux thermes de Bath, mais également à la ville portuaire de Bristol et ainsi, au Pays de Galle et à l'Irlande, fut créée par l'occupant romain comme route de transport pour les troupes et la relève. Les Romains étaient des constructeurs de route expérimentés et c'est pour cette raison qu'ils surélevèrent cette route importante, et la construisirent bombée, afin que l'eau de pluie puisse s'écouler.

BUCKINGHAM PALACE, AT THE TIME OF THE RESIDENCE OF KING GEORGE IV

INK AND WATERCOLOR BY AUGUSTUS CHARLES PUGIN, 1827

Compared to other royal palaces, Buckingham Palace is not that old. It was built as a private residence in 1702 for the Duke of Buckingham, the illegitimate son of King James II. It has been much altered and remodeled over the years, beginning with George III in 1762. In 1820, George IV hired the famous architect John Nash (responsible also for the Nash terraced houses in Regent's Park and the Royal Pavilion in Brighton) to rebuild the palace with a three-sided court open to the east, facing the Mall and Trafalgar Square. In 1830, the newly married Queen Victoria appointed the architect Edward Blore to enclose the courtyard.

Buckingham Palace is flanked by St. James's Park and Marlborough House (the former home of Queen Elizabeth II's grandmother), Clarence House (the former home of the Queen Mother), St. James's Palace (the London home of Price Charles), Lancaster House, and Green Park. The palace is approached along the Mall as you pass under Admiralty Arch from Trafalgar Square.

Buckingham Palace is the London home of Queen Elizabeth II and her family when she is not staying at Windsor Castle, Sandringham Estate, or Balmoral Castle.

BUCKINGHAM PALACE, ZUR ZEIT DER RESIDENZ KÖNIG GEORGE IV.

TUSCHE UND AQUARELL VON AUGUSTUS CHARLES PUGIN, 1827

Verglichen mit anderen königlichen Palästen ist der Buckingham Palace noch nicht sehr alt. Er wurde als privater Wohnsitz für den Herzog von Buckingham, einen illegitimen Sohn König James II., im Jahr 1702 erbaut. George III. begann 1762 mit dem Umbau und der Neugestaltung des Hauses. 1820 beauftragte George IV. den bekannten Architekten John Nash, der unter anderem für die Nash Reihenhäuser am Regent's Park und den Royal Pavilion in Brighton verantwortlich war, den Palast mit einem Innenhof zu versehen: Er wird von drei Flügeln eingefasst und öffnet sich nach Osten zu Mall und Trafalgar Square. 1830 engagierte die frisch verheiratete Königin Victoria den Architekten Edward Blore, den Abschluss der Arbeiten vorzunehmen.

Flankiert wird der Buckingham Palace an den Seiten vom St. James's Park und dem Marlborough House (dem ehemaligen Wohnhaus der Großmutter von Elizabeth II.), dem Clarence House (dem ehemaligen Wohnhaus der Königin Mutter), dem St. James Palace (der heutigen Londoner Residenz von Prinz Charles), dem Lancaster House und dem Green Park. Vom Trafalgar Square aus kommend geht man entlang der Mall unter der Admirality Arch hindurch auf den Palast zu.

Der Buckingham Palace ist die Londoner Residenz von Königin Elizabeth II. und ihrer Familie, sofern sie sich nicht in Windsor Castle, Sandringham Estate oder Balmoral Castle aufhält.

BUCKINGHAM PALACE, À L'ÉPOQUE RÉSIDENCE DU ROI GEORGES IV

ENCRE DE CHINE ET AQUARELLE D'AUGUSTUS CHARLES PUGIN, 1827

Comparé à d'autres palais royaux, Buckingham Palace n'est encore pas très ancien. Il fut édifié comme résidence privée pour le duc de Buckingham, un fils illégitime du roi Jacques II, en 1702. En 1762, Georges III fit commencer des travaux et la nouvelle conception de la maison. En 1820, George IV confia au célèbre architecte John Nash, à qui l'on doit, entre autres, les Terraces au Regent's Park et le Royal Pavilion à Brighton, de munir le palais d'une cour intérieure : elle est encadrée de trois ailes et s'ouvre vers l'est sur le Mall et Trafalgar Square. En 1830, la reine Victoria, jeune mariée, engagea l'architecte Edward Blore pour mener à bien les travaux.

Buckingham Palace est flanqué de St. James's Park et de Marlborough House (l'ancienne demeure de la grand-mère d'Élisabeth II), de Clarence House (l'ancienne demeure de la reine Mère), de St. James Palace (l'actuelle résidence londonienne du prince Charles), de Lancaster House et de Green Park. En venant de Trafalgar Square, on passe sous l'Admirality Arch, le long du Mall, pour se diriger vers le palais.

Buckingham Palace est la résidence londonienne de la reine Élisabeth II et de sa famille, lorsqu'elle ne séjourne pas au château de Windsor Castle, à Sandringham Estate ou au château de Balmoral.

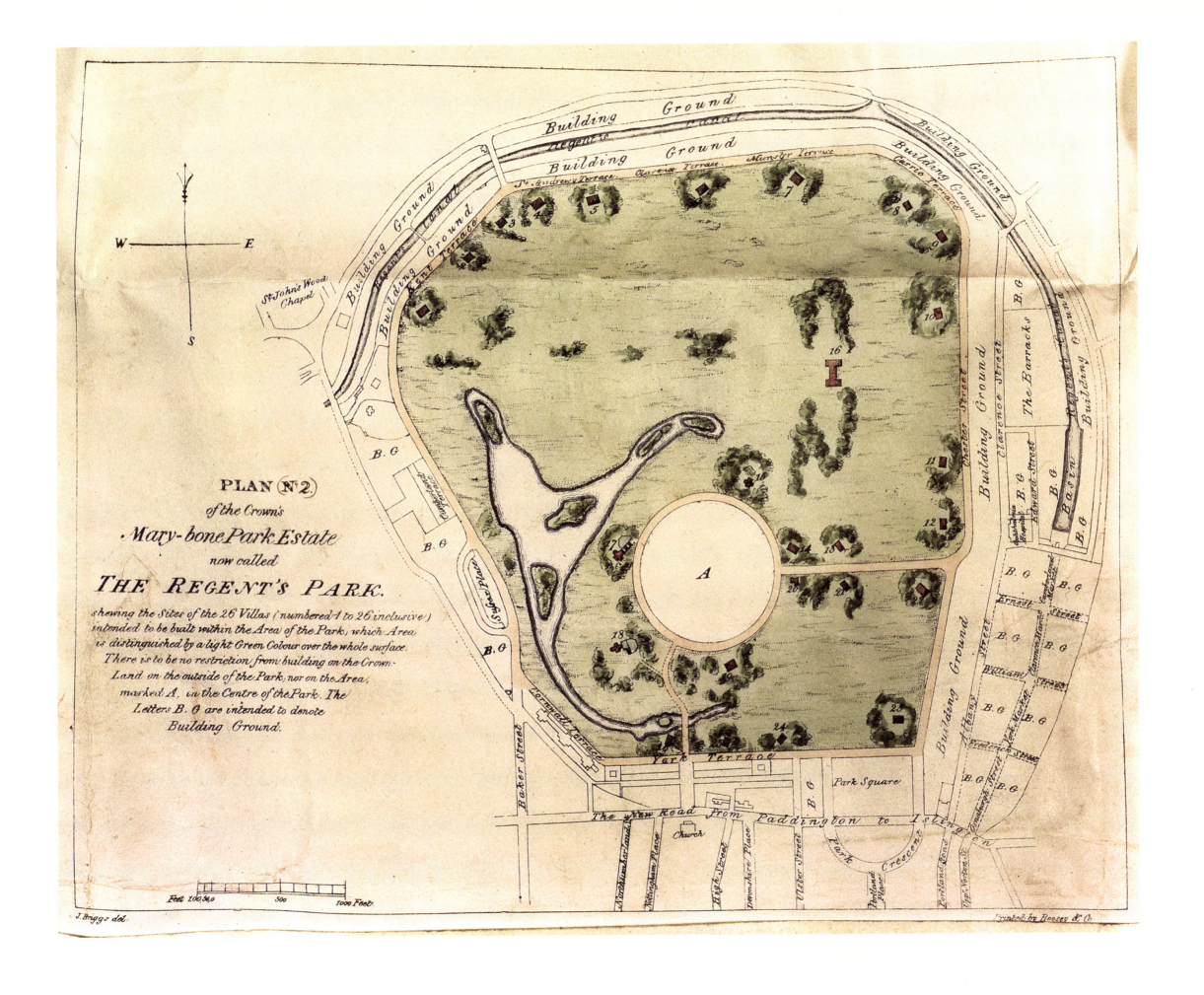

Plan of Regent's Park, 1822

DRAWN BY J. BRIGGS AND PRINTED BY
BOOSEY & CO.

Beginning in 1811, the architect John Nash designed and built Piccadilly Circus (originally Regent Circus), Regent Street, Oxford Circus, Portland Place, and finally, Cumberland Terrace and Chester Terrace. Regent Street was the brainchild of the prince regent (the heir to George IV), who envisioned a "Royal Mile", after the magnificent boulevards of Napoleon's Paris. The grand street was to run from his official residence at Carlton House to his summerhouse in the park.

Regent's Park was planned in 1822. The Zoological Gardens (now London Zoo) was added at a later date to replace the Menagerie that was founded in medieval times by King Henry III as a tourist attraction.

During the winter many people skated on the pond in Regent's Park. However, disaster struck in January 1867 when the ice broke and forty-one people drowned as thousands stood helplessly on the banks. New regulations were introduced for London's parks that forbid skating unless the ice was five inches thick.

Plan von Regent's Park, 1822

GEZEICHNET VON J. BRIGGS, GEDRUCKT
VON BOOSEY & CO.

Ab 1811 entwarf und baute der Architekt John Nash Picadilly Circus (ursprünglich Regent Circus), Regent Street, Oxford Circus, Portland Place, Cumberland Terrace und Chester Terrace. Die Regent Street wurde nach einer Idee des Prinzregenten (des späteren Königs George IV.) entworfen, der sich eine »Royal Mile«, eine königliche Zeremonienstraße nach dem Vorbild der Boulevards Napoleons in Paris wünschte. Diese Flaniermeile sollte von seiner offiziellen Residenz, dem Carlton House, bis zu seiner Sommerresidenz im Park führen.

Der Regent's Park wurde 1822 entworfen. Der Zoologische Garten (heute Londoner Zoo) wurde später hinzugefügt und ersetzte die Menagerie, die im Mittelalter von König Henry III. als Touristenattraktion erbaut wurde.

Vor allem im Winter war der See im Regent's Park eine Attraktion für Eisläufer. Als jedoch im Jahr 1867 das Eis einbrach und Tausende vom Ufer des Sees hilflos zusehen mussten, wie 41 Menschen starben, wurde für die Londoner Parks eine neue Vorschrift erlassen, die das Eislaufen verbietet, wenn das Eis nicht eine Mindestdicke von dreizehn Zentimetern hat.

Plan de Regent's Park, 1822

DESSINÉ PAR J. BRIGGS, IMPRIMÉ PAR
BOOSEY & CO.

À partir de 1811, l'architecte John Nash conçut et bâtit Piccadilly Circus (à l'origine, Regent Circus), Regent Street, Oxford Circus, Portland Place, Cumberland Terrace et Chester Terrace. Regent Street fut conçue d'après une idée du prince régent (le futur roi Georges IV), qui souhaitait une « Royal Mile », une avenue de cérémonie royale selon l'exemple des boulevards de Napoléon à Paris. Cette promenade devait mener de sa résidence officielle, Carlton House, à sa résidence estivale dans le parc.

Regent's Park fut conçu en 1822. Le Jardin zoologique (actuel zoo de Londres) fut ajouté par la suite et remplaça la ménagerie qui avait été édifiée au Moyen Âge par le roi Henri III d'Angleterre.

Le lac de Regent's Park était avant tout une attraction en hiver pour les patineurs. Cependant, lorsque, en 1867, la glace se rompit et que depuis la rive, des milliers de gens impuissants assistèrent à la noyade de 41 personnes, un nouveau règlement pour les parcs londoniens fut promulgué, interdisant le patinage, tant que la glace n'avait pas atteint une épaisseur de treize centimètres au minimum.

SURVEY OF THE ROYAL PALACE OF KENSINGTON FOR HER MAJESTY, ANNE, QUEEN OF GREAT BRITAIN, FRANCE, AND IRELAND (1702–1714)

ENGRAVING BY JOHANNES KIP, 1730
(AFTER A LEONARD KNYFF ENGRAVING)

When William III of Orange (a Dutch prince) and Queen Mary (the daughter of King James II) ascended to the throne in 1689, William was most unhappy with the royal residence of St. James's Palace. In order to provide a suitable home for the royal family, he commissioned Sir Christopher Wren to significantly enlarge a private house that he had purchased. He had acquired the house, along with twenty-six acres of land in the village of Kensington, from Lord Nottingham for twenty thousand pounds. Unfortunately, Mary died of smallpox in 1694, just four years after Kensington Palace was completed. William died there eight years later after a fall from his horse.

On her succession in 1702, Queen Anne significantly increased the grounds, as is depicted in this view, by adding one hundred acres. The Serpentine Lake (not shown on the survey) was added in 1730 so the royal family could sail pleasure boats.

It is clear from the survey that Queen Anne expanded the palace to be a lavish place. Diana, Princess of Wales, was resident at Kensington Palace until her death in 1997, and her official memorial is located in the park.

ÜBERSICHT ÜBER DEN KÖNIGLICHEN PALAST VON KENSINGTON FÜR IHRE MAJESTÄT, ANNE, KÖNIGIN VON GROSSBRITANNIEN, FRANKREICH UND IRLAND (1702–1714)

KUPFERSTICH VON JOHANNES KIP, 1730
(NACH EINEM KUPFERSTICH VON LEONARD KNYFF)

Als Wilhelm III. von Oranien-Nassau und Königin Mary von England (Tochter von König James II.) 1689 den Thron bestiegen, befand Wilhelm die königliche Residenz, den St. James Palace, als unzureichend für seine Bedürfnisse, und so beauftragte er Sir Christopher Wren, eine geeignete Residenz für die königliche Familie zu entwerfen. Zu diesem Zweck erwarb Wilhelm III. von Lord Nottingham ein Privathaus mit dazugehörigen zehn Hektar Grundbesitz in Kensington für zwanzigtausend Pfund. Nur vier Jahre nachdem der Kensington Palace fertig gestellt war, verstarb Mary im Jahr 1694 an Pocken. Wilhelm starb dort acht Jahre später nach einem Sturz von seinem Pferd.

Als Königin Anne 1702 die Nachfolge antrat, vergrößerte sie den Grundbesitz noch einmal um weitere 40 Hektar. 1730 wurde der Serpentine Lake angelegt (in der Ansicht nicht abgebildet), so dass die königliche Familie auch Boot fahren konnte.

Aus der Übersicht lässt sich erkennen, dass der Palast unter Königin Anne zu einem großzügigen Besitz erweitert wurde. Diana, Prinzessin von Wales, residierte bis zu ihrem Tod im Jahr 1997 im Kensington Palace; die offizielle Gedenkstätte für die Prinzessin befindet sich im dortigen Park.

VUE DU PALAIS ROYAL DE KENSINGTON POUR SA MAJESTÉ, ANNE, REINE DE GRANDE-BRETAGNE, DE FRANCE ET D'IRLANDE (1702–1714)

GRAVURE SUR CUIVRE DE JOHANNES KIP, 1730
(D'APRÈS UNE GRAVURE SUR CUIVRE DE LEONARD KNYFF)

Lorsque Guillaume III d'Orange-Nassau et la reine Marie II d'Angleterre (fille du roi Jacques II) montèrent sur le trône en 1689, Guillaume trouva que la résidence royale, le St. James Palace, ne correspondait pas à ses besoins. Il chargea alors Sir Christopher Wren de concevoir une résidence adéquate pour la famille royale. À cet effet, Guillaume acquit auprès de Lord Nottingham une demeure avec une propriété de dix hectares à Kensington pour la somme de vingt mille livres. Quatre ans seulement après que Kensington Palace eut été achevé, Marie II décéda en 1694 de la variole. Guillaume y mourut huit ans plus tard des suites d'une chute de cheval.

Lorsque la reine Anne leur succéda en 1702, elle agrandit la propriété de 40 hectares supplémentaires. En 1730, le Serpentine Lake fut aménagé (non représenté sur la vue), afin que la famille royale puisse aussi faire du bateau.

La vue permet de reconnaître que le palais, sous la reine Anne, était devenu une vaste propriété. Diana, princesse de Galles, a résidé jusqu'à sa mort en 1997 au Kensington Palace ; le monument commémoratif qui lui est dédié se trouve dans le parc.

THE CRYSTAL PALACE

LITHOGRAPH OF THE GREAT EXHIBITION, 1851

Originally built to house the Great Exhibition of the Works of Industry of All Nations in 1851, the Crystal Palace, as it was called, was considered the architectural marvel of its age. The building, constructed of delicate cast iron and covered with three hundred thousand panes of glass, covered a full nineteen acres of Hyde Park. The exhibition galleries totaled nearly two miles and in some places stood over one hundred feet in order to accommodate the tall elm trees displayed inside. The Crystal Palace was built in just four months using nine hundred thousand square feet of glass. Some panes were four feet long and one foot wide. The strength of the building was tested by pulling eight-ton carts filled with cannonballs up and down the galleries, and marching soldiers around the building in close formation. When Queen Victoria opened the exhibition, complete with more than one hundred thousand exhibits, on May 1, 1851, twenty-five thousand people filled the building.

In the five months it was open, the exhibition attracted six million people, equal to one-third of the population. The Crystal Palace was reerected in South London and remained open for exhibitions and entertainment until it burned to the ground in 1936.

DER CRYSTAL PALACE

LITHOGRAPHIE DER LONDONER INDUSTRIEAUSSTELLUNG, 1851

Ursprünglich erbaut als Ausstellungsgebäude für die Londoner Industrieausstellung 1851, wurde der Crystal Palace als architektonisches Wunderwerk seiner Zeit gefeiert. Das Gebäude, aus filigranen Gusseisenteilen konstruiert und mit 300 000 Glasscheiben bedeckt, erstreckte sich über eine Gesamtfläche von 7,5 Hektar im Hyde Park. Die Ausstellungsgalerien bilden eine Strecke von fast 3,5 Kilometern und waren an manchen Stellen über dreißig Meter hoch, um Platz für die hohen Ulmenbäume im Inneren zu schaffen. Der Bau des Crystal Palace dauerte nur vier Monate, es wurden über 83 000 Quadratmeter Glas verbaut, wobei manche Glasscheiben 120 mal 30 Zentimeter groß waren. Um die Festigkeit des Gebäudes zu testen, wurden acht Tonnen schwere, mit Kanonenkugeln beladene Wagen quer über die Galerien gezogen, und Soldaten marschierten in enger Formation rund um das Gebäude. Bei der Eröffnung der Ausstellung durch Königin Victoria am 1. Mai 1851 hielten sich 25 000 Menschen im Gebäude auf.

Während ihrer fünfmonatigen Öffnungszeit lockte die Ausstellung, die über einhunderttausend Exponate präsentierte, mehr als sechs Millionen Menschen an, was einem Drittel der damaligen Bevölkerung entspricht. Der Crystal Palace wurde im Süden der Stadt wieder aufgebaut und für Ausstellungen und Veranstaltungen genutzt, bis er 1936 vollständig niederbrannte.

LE CRYSTAL PALACE

LITHOGRAPHIE DE L'EXPOSITION INDUSTRIELLE DE LONDRES, 1851

Construit à l'origine comme pavillon pour l'Exposition industrielle de Londres en 1851, le Crystal Palace fut acclamé comme une merveille architecturale de son époque. Le bâtiment, composé d'une structure en fer forgé filigrane, et recouvert de 300 000 vitres, s'étendait sur une superficie totale de 7,5 hectares dans Hyde Park. Les galeries d'exposition formaient un trajet de presque 3,5 kilomètres et à certains endroits, atteignaient plus de trente mètres de hauteur afin de permettre d'abriter les grands ormes à l'intérieur. La construction du Crystal Palace ne dura que quatre mois, plus de 83 000 mètres carrés de verre ont été utilisés, certaines vitres mesurant 120 centimètres par 30. Afin de tester la solidité du bâtiment, des voitures de huit tonnes, chargées de boulets de canon, furent tirées à travers les galeries, et des soldats défilèrent en rangs serrés autour du pavillon. Lors de l'inauguration de l'exposition par la reine Victoria le 1er mai 1851, 25 000 personnes se tenaient dans le bâtiment.

Pendant les cinq mois que dura l'exposition, qui présentait plus de cent mille pièces, elle attira plus de six millions de personnes, ce qui correspond à un tiers de la population d'alors.

Le Crystal Palace fut reconstruit au sud de la ville et utilisé pour des expositions et des manifestations, jusqu'à ce qu'il soit totalement ravagé par un incendie en 1936.

WESTMINSTER BRIDGE, THE HOUSES OF PARLIAMENT, AND WESTMINSTER ABBEY

OIL ON CANVAS BY JOHN McVICAR ANDERSON, 1872, SIGNED AND DATED

This moonlit view shows the Houses of Parliament, with their long river frontage, flanked by Victoria Tower on the far side and the Clock Tower (affectionately know as Big Ben and likely named after the commissioner of works at the time). St. Stephen's Hall, once used as one of the Houses of Parliament, is the middle tower. Westminster Bridge, seen in the foreground, is the replacement for the original bridge built in the mid-eighteenth century. The disastrous fire of 1834 destroyed most of the historic Palace of Westminster, except Westminster Hall. The neo-Gothic design of the new Houses of Parliament was the creation of Augustus Pugin and established a new concept in design among leading architects of the time. The building was completed in 1860.
Westminster Abbey and the early Tudor parish church of St. Margaret's at its rear are shown to the right. Westminster Abbey, built by the Saxons under Edward the Confessor, was completed in 1065 and became the location for the coronation of the kings and queens of England and the burial place for many of its royal and noble subjects.

WESTMINSTER BRIDGE, HOUSE OF PARLIAMENT UND WESTMINSTER ABBEY

ÖL AUF LEINWAND VON JOHN McVICAR ANDERSON, 1872, SIGNIERT UND DATIERT

Die in Mondlicht getauchte Ansicht zeigt das House of Parliament mit der langen Flussfront, flankiert vom Victoria Tower auf der abgewandten Seite und dem Uhrturm (liebevoll auch Big Ben genannt und wahrscheinlich nach dem damaligen Hauptverantwortlichen der Bauarbeiten benannt). Der mittlere Turm, der einst als Parlamentsgebäude genutzt wurde, ist die St. Stephen's Hall. Die Westminster Bridge im Vordergrund ist Mitte des 18. Jahrhunderts als Ersatz für die ursprüngliche Brücke neu gebaut worden.
Ein katastrophales Feuer zerstörte 1834 einen Großteil des historischen Westminster Palastes, nicht aber die Westminster Hall. Das neue Parlamentsgebäude im neugotischen Stil wurde von Augustus Pugin entworfen und 1860 fertig gestellt und begründete unter den zu dieser Zeit führenden Architekten ein neues Designkonzept. In der Ansicht sieht man die 1065 unter Edward dem Bekenner errichtete Westminster Abbey, die festlicher Schauplatz der Krönungen der Könige und Königinnen Englands war sowie Begräbnisstätte vieler ihrer königlichen und adeligen Untertanen wurde, rechts dahinter die Pfarrkirche St. Margret's im Tudorstil.

WESTMINSTER BRIDGE, HOUSE OF PARLIAMENT ET WESTMINSTER ABBEY

HUILE SUR TOILE DE JOHN McVICAR ANDERSON, 1872, SIGNÉE ET DATÉE

La vue baignée de clair de lune montre la House of Parliament, avec sa longue façade sur le fleuve, flanquée de la Victoria Tower de l'autre côté, et le clocher (nommé aussi avec affection Big Ben, probablement d'après le responsable des travaux jadis). La tour au centre, qui fut autrefois attribuée au Parlement, est St. Stephen's Hall. Westminster Bridge, au premier plan, a été construit au milieu du XVIIIᵉ siècle pour remplacer le pont d'origine. Un incendie catastrophique détruisit en 1834 une grande partie du palais historique de Westminster, épargnant Westminster Hall. Le nouveau bâtiment du Parlement de style néo-gothique fut conçu par Augustus Pugin et achevé en 1860. Il fut à l'origine d'un nouveau courant parmi les architectes de pointe de cette époque.
Sur la vue, on voit Westminster Abbey, édifiée en 1065 sous Édouard le Confesseur, qui fut le théâtre des cérémonies du couronnement des rois et reines d'Angleterre, ainsi que le lieu de sépulture de bon nombre de leurs sujets royaux et nobles ; derrière, à droite, l'église paroissiale St. Margret's de style Tudor.

A Tribute to
Sir Christopher Wren

WATERCOLOR PAINTING BY CHARLES ROBERT
COCKERELL, 1870

Sir Christopher Wren was appointed joint head of a group
of six commissioners to redesign the city after the Great
Fire of London in 1666. Although his own radical plan for
the city was rejected, he still designed and supervised the
rebuilding of fifty-one of the eighty-nine new churches,
including St. Paul's Cathedral. Although it took twenty-
one years to rebuild St. Paul's, the speed with which Wren
rebuilt parts of London was remarkable. Most of the
churches were rebuilt in sixteen years, beginning in 1670.
75 percent of the city had been rebuilt within five years.
The view sets out to create a collage of the churches Wren
rebuilt and to salute his greatest achievement, St. Paul's
Cathedral.

Ein Tribut an
Sir Christopher Wren

AQUARELL VON CHARLES ROBERT COCKERELL,
1870

Sir Christopher Wren war Leiter einer aus sechs Mitglie-
dern bestehenden Kommission für den Wiederaufbau
der Stadt nach dem Großen Brand von London 1666.
Obwohl sein eigener radikaler Plan abgelehnt wurde,
entwarf und leitete er den Wiederaufbau von 51 der 89
neuen Kirchen, darunter auch der St. Paul's Cathedral.
Ab 1670 wurde innerhalb von sechzehn Jahren ein Großteil der Kirchen wieder aufgebaut, und fünfundsiebzig
Prozent der City von London waren nach fünf Jahren
wieder hergestellt.
Dieses Bild stellt eine Collage der von Wren wieder
erbauten Kirchen dar und ehrt sein größtes Werk, die
St. Paul's Cathedral.

Un hommage à
Sir Christopher Wren

AQUARELLE DE CHARLES ROBERT COCKERELL,
1870

Sir Christopher Wren était directeur d'une commission
formée de six membres, qui avait été chargée de la
reconstruction de la ville après le Grand Incendie de
1666. Bien que son propre plan radical ait été refusé, il
conçut et dirigea la reconstruction de 51 des 89 nouvelles
églises, parmi lesquelles figurait aussi la cathédrale Saint-
Paul. À partir de 1670, en l'espace de seize années, une
grande partie des églises avait été reconstruite, et soixante-
quinze pour cent de la City de Londres avaient déjà été
rebâtis.
Ce tableau est un collage des églises reconstruites par
Wren, et rend hommage à sa plus grande œuvre, St. Paul's
Cathedral.

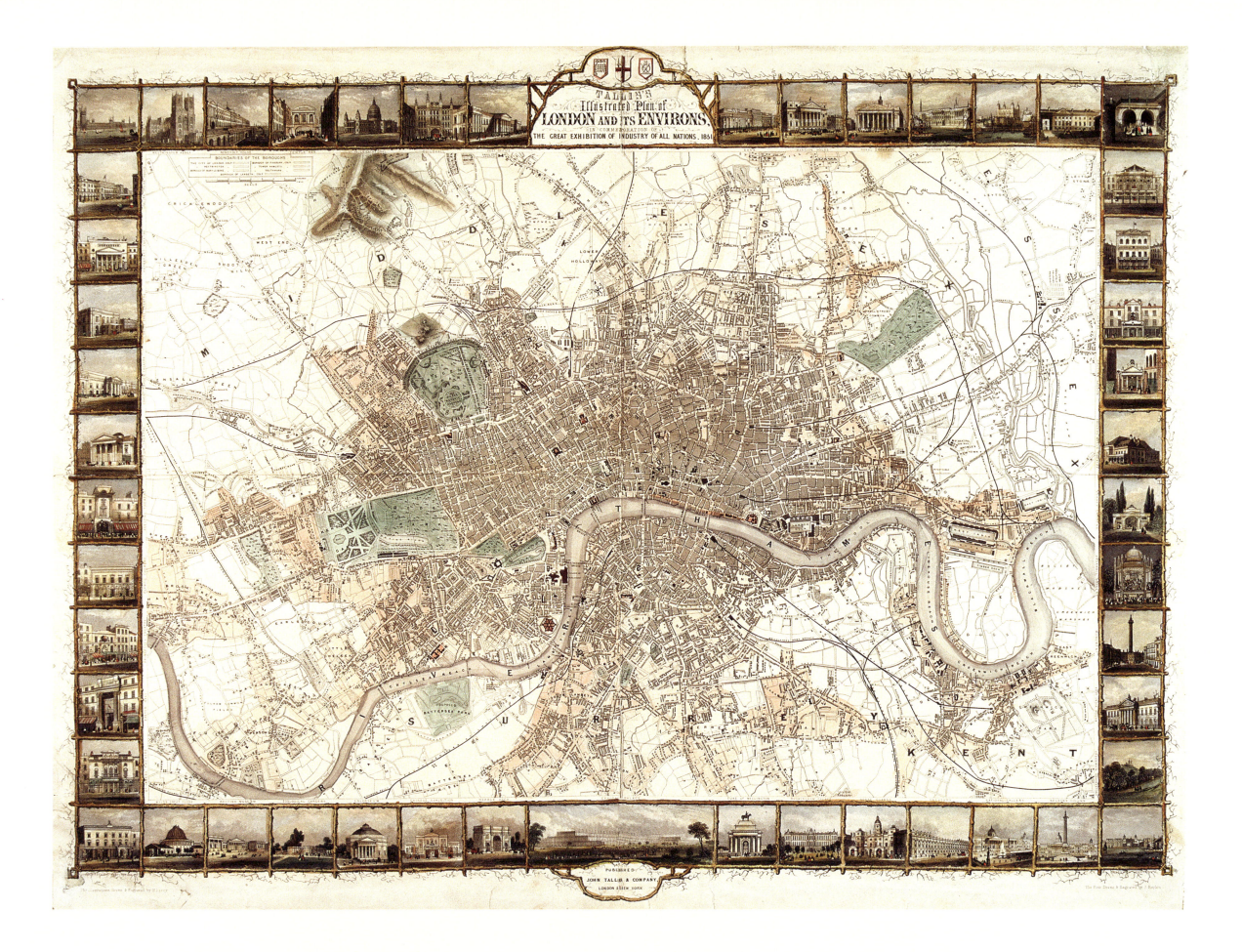

MAP OF LONDON IN COMMEMORATION OF THE GREAT EXHIBITION OF INDUSTRY OF ALL NATIONS, 1851

ENGRAVING BY JOHN TALLIS & CO, 1851.
RELEASED AS A FOLDING MAP OF LONDON

The Great Exhibition of Industry of All Nations was held in Hyde Park under the glass exhibition building known as the Crystal Palace. Queen Victoria's husband, the prince consort, was president of the event, a show of many different industrial displays with more than one hundred thousand exhibits. Six million people, many from overseas, attended the Great Exhibition.
The idea of this map was to furnish visitors with a folded guide to London as well as a souvenir of the wonderful places and buildings they may have seen while visiting. The border consists of forty-nine views "of all the Public Buildings and Places of Amusement in the British Metropolis and its suburbs." Such views include theatres, parks, the Zoological Gardens, museums, and other places of entertainment and interest.

GEDENKKARTE LONDONS ANLÄSSLICH DER LONDONER INDUSTRIE-AUSSTELLUNG, 1851

KUPFERSTICH VON JOHN TALLIS & CO, 1851,
ERSCHIENEN ALS FALTKARTE LONDONS

Die Londoner Industrieausstellung fand im Hyde Park in einem verglasten Gebäude statt, das als Crystal Palace bekannt wurde. Der Prinzgemahl, Königin Victorias Ehemann, übernahm die Schirmherrschaft der Veranstaltung, die mehr als einhunderttausend Exponate aus verschiedenen Industriezweigen zeigte. Sechs Millionen Besucher kamen zur Londoner Industrieausstellung, darunter auch viele aus Übersee.
Das Ziel dieser Karte war es, den Besuchern einen faltbaren Stadtführer zur Verfügung zu stellen, der auch gleichzeitig eine kleine Erinnerung an die in London besuchten Orte und Gebäude war.
Auf dem Rand werden 49 Ansichten »aller öffentlichen Gebäude und Veranstaltungsorte in der britischen Metropole und ihrer Vorstädte« gezeigt. Bilder von Theatern, Parks, dem Zoologischen Garten, Museen und anderen Veranstaltungsorten und Sehenswürdigkeiten befinden sich darunter.

CARTE COMMÉMORATIVE DE LONDRES À L'OCCASION DE L'EXPOSITION INDUSTRIELLE DE 1851

GRAVURE SUR CUIVRE DE JOHN TALLIS & CO, 1851, PARUE COMME PLAN PLIÉ DE LONDRES

L'Exposition industrielle de Londres se déroula à Hyde Park dans un bâtiment en verre, connu sous le nom de Crystal Palace. Le prince consort, mari de la reine Victoria, accepta le patronage de la manifestation, qui montrait plus de cent mille pièces d'exposition de différentes branches de l'industrie. Six millions de visiteurs, parmi lesquels ceux d'outre-mer étaient nombreux aussi, se rendirent à l'Exposition industrielle de Londres.
Cette carte avait pour but de présenter aux visiteurs un plan de la ville plié, qui était aussi un petit souvenir des endroits et des monuments visités à Londres.
Tout autour, 49 vues de « l'ensemble des bâtiments publics et lieux de manifestations dans la métropole britannique et ses banlieues ». Des reproductions de théâtres, de parcs, du jardin zoologique, des musées et d'autres lieux culturels et monuments y figurent.

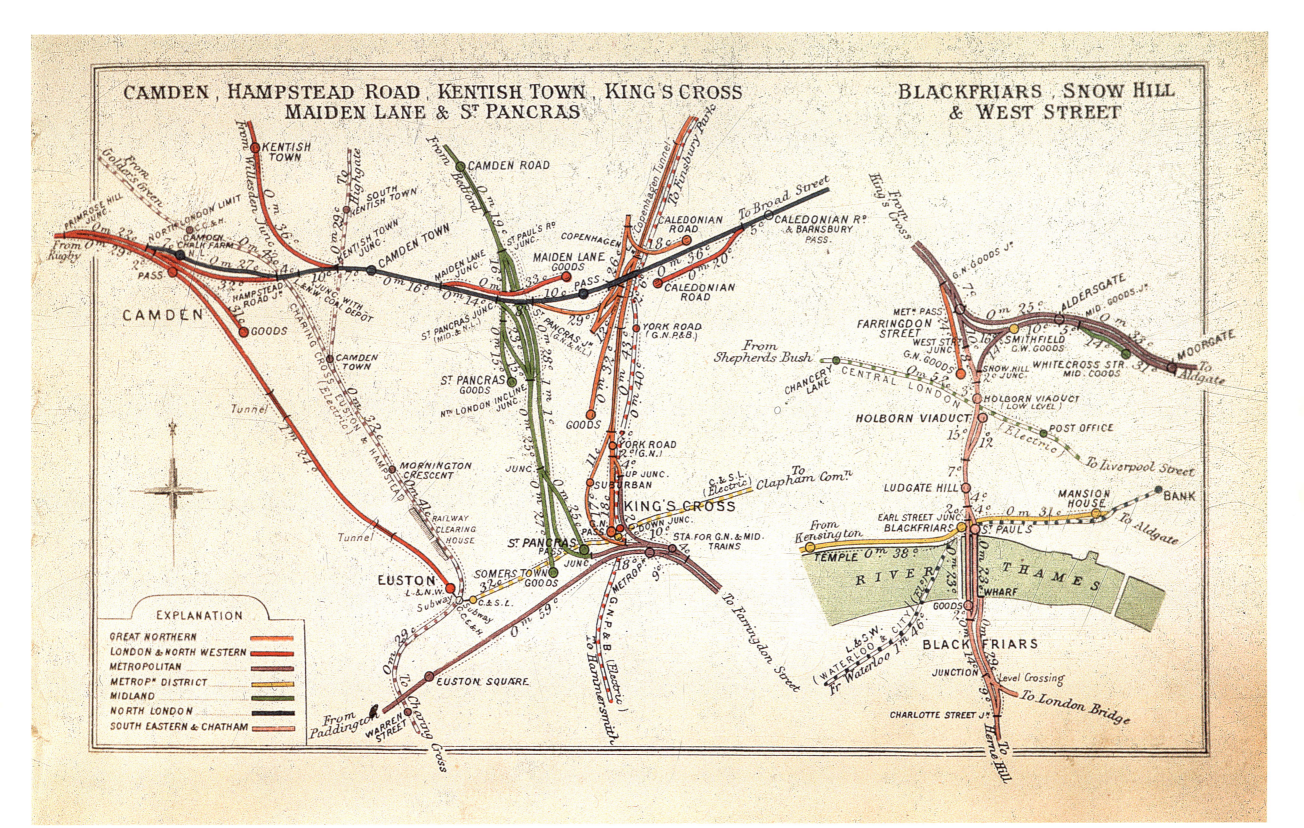

EARLY MAP OF THE LONDON UNDERGROUND

ENGRAVED, C. 1880

This color lithograph from the late nineteenth century shows the early stages of the London Underground. The world's first underground track opened in London in 1863 as part of the Metropolitan Railway from Paddington to Farringdon Street, near St. Paul's Cathedral, and was used for freight services. The Underground Service was founded in 1870 when the underground system began to be used for passenger services. Electric trains were introduced to replace steam engines, and the term "rush hour" came into being as a result of the heavy use at the beginning of each workday. The Underground became known commonly as the Tube, after the introduction of the Twopenny Tube Central Line in 1900.

In the early days the Underground routes were marked as overlays on existing maps. Before long, routes were represented on the map as color-coded lines connecting each of the stations, which eliminated extraneous detail. By 1912, the Underground Service was under the control of the Underground Electric Railways Company, and in 1933, the coordination passed to London Transport along with the oversight of buses, coaches, and trams. Today the Underground carries 3 million passengers every weekday, has 255 miles of subway lines, and connects more than 360 stations.

London Transport and the British government installed floodgates at major stations at the beginning of World War II as emergency antiflooding measures were taken on the north side of the Thames River. The stations and tunnels were used as bomb shelters during World War II. It was estimated that 175,000 people took nightly cover in the deep subterranean tube stations.

FRÜHE KARTE DES LONDONER U-BAHNNETZES

KUPFERSTICH, UM 1880

Dieser Farbstich aus dem späten 19. Jahrhundert zeigt die Anfänge des Londoner U-Bahnsystems. Die weltweit erste U-Bahnstrecke, die zuerst ausschließlich dem Güterverkehr vorenthalten war, wurde in London 1863 als Teil der Metropolitan Railway von Paddington zur Farrington Street nahe der St. Paul's Cathedral eröffnet. Der U-Bahndienst wurde 1870 gegründet, als man das unterirdische Bahnsystem auch zum Fahrgasttransport einsetzte. Der eingeführte Elektroantrieb ersetzte die Dampfloks, und der Begriff der »rush hour« entstand, weil die Züge besonders morgens vor Arbeitsbeginn stark frequentiert waren. Seit der Eröffnung der Twopenny Tube Central Line im Jahr 1900 wurde aus der Underground die Tube.

In den Anfangstagen der U-Bahn wurden die Strecken einfach auf bereits vorhandene Karten gedruckt. Kurze Zeit später markierten farbige Linien die Verbindung zwischen den Stationen, wodurch belanglose Informationen nicht mehr auftauchten. Um 1912 war der U-Bahndienst der Underground Electric Railways Company unterstellt, 1933 übernahm die London Transport dann die Oberaufsicht über den U-Bahn-, Bus- und Bahnverkehr. Werktags transportiert die U-Bahn heute drei Millionen Passagiere, das Streckennetz verbindet 360 Haltestellen auf 410 Kilometern.

Zu Beginn des Zweiten Weltkriegs installierten die London Transport und die britische Regierung in den Hauptbahnhöfen Hochwasserklappen, da Hochwasserschutzarbeiten an der Nordseite der Themse ausgeführt wurden. Die Bahnhöfe und Tunnel wurden zudem während des Zweiten Weltkriegs als Bunker genutzt und die Zahl der Menschen, die über Nacht in den tief unter der Erde liegenden U-Bahnstationen Schutz suchten, wurde auf 175 000 geschätzt.

ANCIENNE CARTE DU RÉSEAU MÉTROPOLITAIN LONDONIEN

GRAVURE SUR CUIVRE, VERS 1880

Cette gravure en couleur de la fin du XIXe siècle montre les débuts du réseau du métropolitain londonien. La première ligne de métro du monde, qui était tout d'abord réservée au transport des marchandises, fut inaugurée à Londres en 1863, c'était une partie du Metropolitan Railway allant de Paddington à Farrington Street, proche de St. Paul's Cathedral. Le métro fut fondé en 1870, lorsque le réseau souterrain fut également affecté au transport des voyageurs. La propulsion à l'électricité remplaça la locomotive à vapeur, et le terme de « rush hour » fit son apparition, car les trains étaient très fréquentés surtout le matin, avant le début du travail. À partir de l'ouverture de la ligne Twopenny Tube Central Line en 1900, l'Underground devint le Tube .

Au cours des premiers jours du métro, les correspondances furent simplement imprimées sur les cartes déjà existantes. Peu après, les lignes en couleur marquaient les correspondances entre les stations, les informations inintéressantes n'apparaissant plus. Vers 1912, le réseau du métro dépendait de la compagnie Underground Electric Railways, en 1933, London Transport reprit ensuite le contrôle du trafic du métro, du bus et du train. Les jours ouvrables, le métro transporte aujourd'hui trois millions de passagers, les correspondances relient 360 stations sur 410 kilomètres.

Au début de la Seconde Guerre mondiale, London Transport et le gouvernement britannique installèrent des portes anti-inondations dans les gares principales, des mesures de protection contre les crues étant effectuées du côté nord de la Tamise. Les gares et les tunnels ont été de surcroît utilisés comme abris pendant la Seconde Guerre mondiale, et le nombre de personnes qui ont cherché refuge dans les stations de métro situées loin sous terre, est estimé à 175 000.

THE WONDERGROUND MAP
OF LONDON TOWN

COLOR PRINT OF THE OVERGROUND MAP OF
LONDON. DRAWING BY MACDONALD GILL, C. 1915

This tourist map showing the attractions of the city and
the location of the Underground stations provided direction for travelers on trams, electric trains (the Underground), and motor-driven buses. The map covers the
eight boroughs that made up the center of London at the
beginning of the twentieth century.
With more and more citizens commuting from the suburbs
to the city during this period, there was rapid growth in
the use of public transportation. Adding to this growth
was also a great need for the transport of people displaced
by enemy bombing during World War I.

WONDERGROUND MAP
OF LONDON TOWN

FARBDRUCK DES LONDONER STADTPLANS,
ZEICHNUNG VON MACDONALD GILL, UM 1915

Diese Touristenkarte zeigt die Sehenswürdigkeiten der
Stadt und die Lage der U-Bahnstationen und liefert so
Wegbeschreibungen für Reisende, die das Straßenbahn-,
U-Bahn- und Bussystem nutzen wollten. Die Karte umfasst die acht Bezirke, die am Anfang des 20. Jahrhunderts
im Zentrum Londons lagen.
Da immer mehr Menschen zu dieser Zeit aus den Vor-
städten in die Stadt pendelten, stieg die Nutzung der
öffentlichen Verkehrsmittel stetig an und wurde für die
durch feindliche Bomben vertriebenen Menschen während des Ersten Weltkriegs umso wichtiger.

CARTE WONDERGROUND
DE LA VILLE DE LONDRES

CHROMO DU PLAN DE LA VILLE DE LONDRES,
DESSIN DE MACDONALD GILL, VERS 1915

Cette carte touristique montre les curiosités de la ville
et l'emplacement de stations de métro. Elle livre ainsi les
descriptions de trajets pour les voyageurs qui veulent
utiliser le réseau de trams, de métro et de bus. La carte
comporte les huit districts qui se trouvaient au début du
XXe siècle au centre de Londres.
Comme, à cette époque, de plus en plus de gens faisaient
la navette entre les banlieues et la ville, l'utilisation des
transports en commun s'accrut en permanence, et devint
pour les personnes qui avaient été bombardées au cours
de la Première Guerre mondiale d'autant plus importante.

The Pool of London during the Docklands Air Raids

Painting by Charles Pears, 1940

During World War II, England, and London in particular, was bombed heavily by the German air forces in 1940 and 1941, the period known as the "Blitz." In 1944, enemy V1- and V2-rockets sent from continental Europe and across the English Channel further destroyed vast areas of London.

The majority of the bombing was concentrated in the City (the financial center of London) and in the East End of London, where the docklands were situated, so as to disrupt business, shipping, cross-river links, and the movement of armament supplies. In this stark view the searchlight beams meet above Tower Bridge in search of enemy aircraft, with the East End of London ablaze in the background. An estimated 43,000 civilians were killed during the Blitz.

Der Pool of London während der Luftangriffe auf die Docklands

Gemälde von Charles Pears, 1940

Während des Zweiten Weltkriegs wurde England und insbesondere London von der Deutschen Luftwaffe schwer bombardiert. Besonders der Zeitraum zwischen 1940 und 1941 ging unter der Bezeichnung »Blitz« in die Geschichte ein. 1944 zerstörten von Europa aus abgeschossene V1- und V2-Raketen große Teile Londons. Die Bombenangriffe konzentrierten sich hauptsächlich auf die City, das Finanzzentrum Londons, und auf das East End mit seinen Hafengebieten, da der Handel, der Schiffsverkehr, die Flussverbindungen und der Transport von Waffen unterbrochen werden sollte. In dieser sachlichen Darstellung treffen sich die Suchlichter auf der Suche nach gegnerischen Flugzeugen über der Tower Bridge, im Hintergrund steht das East End in Flammen. Dem »Blitz« fielen etwa 43 000 Zivilisten zum Opfer.

Pool of London pendant un bombardement aérien sur les docks

Tableau de Charles Pears, 1940

Pendant la Seconde Guerre mondiale, l'Angleterre, et surtout Londres, fut sévèrement bombardée par la Luftwaffe. En particulier la période entre 1940 et 1941 entra dans l'histoire sous le nom de « Blitz ». En 1944, les missiles V1 et V2, tirées depuis l'Europe, détruisirent de grandes parties de Londres.

Les bombardements se concentraient principalement sur la City, le centre financier de Londres, et sur East End avec ses installations portuaires, car le commerce, le trafic fluvial, les liaisons fluviales et le transport d'armes devaient être interrompus. Dans ce tableau prosaïque, les faisceaux des projecteurs de la défense anti-aérienne se croisent au-dessus de Tower Bridge, à l'arrière-plan, East End est en proie aux flammes. Environ 43 000 civils furent victimes du « Blitz ».

LONDON

BRITAIN

The House of Commons and the House of Lords, together with such adjuncts as Big Ben and historic Westminster Hall, are collectively known as The Palace of Westminster. The present building dates from 1850, its predecessor having been destroyed by fire in 1834; the Chamber of the House of Commons dates from 1950, the former Chamber having been totally destroyed during a bombing attack on 10 May, 1941. Representative government began in Westminster Hall in 1265.

BY GEORGE AYLING, M.R.S.T., S.M.A.

PUBLISHED BY THE BRITISH TRAVEL AND HOLIDAYS ASSOCIATION AND PRINTED IN GREAT BRITAIN BY W. S. COWELL, LTD., AT THE BUTTER MARKET, IPSWICH 54.57.74

The Palace of Westminster and the River Thames

Poster of London by George Ayling, 1954

This poster depicts the House of Commons and the House of Lords, which together with Big Ben, St. Stephen's Church, Westminster Hall, and Victoria Tower are collectively known as the Palace of Westminster. Representative government began in Westminster Hall in 1265 under kings Henry III and Edward I when the Barons demanded reform. It was, however, under Edward III that the House of Commons became more powerful as the king became dependent on Parliament for raising taxes.
After World War II ended in 1945, London struggled as a tourist destination. Much of the city had been badly damaged by air raids and the government lacked resources to rebuild the capital. This poster is an early attempt by the British Travel and Holiday Association Board to attract visitors to London. The House of Commons had recently been rebuilt in 1950 after having been totally destroyed during an enemy aircraft bombing attack in May 1941.

Der Palace of Westminster und die Themse

London-Poster von George Ayling, 1954

Das Poster zeigt das Unterhaus (House of Commons) und Oberhaus (House of Lords), die zusammen mit dem Big Ben, der St. Stephen's Church, der Westminster Hall und dem Victoria Tower unter dem Namen Palace of Westminster bekannt sind. Als 1265 die Barone unter Henry III. und Edward I. Reformen forderten, begannen hier Regierungsvertreter ihre Arbeit aufzunehmen, und damit zog die Demokratie in die Westminster Hall. Die Macht des Unterhauses nahm unter Edward III. zu – auch bei Steuererhöhungen war er nun vom Parlament abhängig. Nach dem Ende des Zweiten Weltkriegs 1945 kämpfte London um seine Stellung als Reiseziel. Ein Großteil der Stadt war bei Luftangriffen stark beschädigt worden, und die Regierung besaß für den Wiederaufbau der Hauptstadt nicht die erforderlichen Mittel. Dieses Poster ist ein erster Versuch des British Travel and Holiday Association Boards, den Tourismus wieder anzukurbeln. Nachdem das Unterhaus während eines Bombenangriffs im Mai 1941 komplett zerstört worden war, wurde es 1950 wieder aufgebaut.

Le palais de Westminster et la Tamise

Affiche de Londres de George Ayling, 1954

L'affiche montre la Chambre des Communes (House of Commons) et la Chambre des Lords (House of Lords) qui, avec Big Ben, St. Stephen's Church, Westminster Hall et Victoria Tower, sont connus sous le nom de Palace of Westminster. Lorsqu'en 1265, les barons réclamèrent des réformes sous Henri III et Edouard Ier, c'est ici que les représentants du gouvernement débutèrent leur travail, et que la démocratie fit son entrée à Westminster Hall. Le pouvoir de la Chambre des Communes augmenta sous Édouard III, même en ce qui concernait les augmentations des impôts, il dépendait à présent du Parlement. À la fin de la Seconde Guerre mondiale en 1945, Londres lutta pour sa position de but de voyage. Une grande partie de la ville avait été fortement endon.magée par les bombardements aériens et le gouvernement ne possédait pas les moyens nécessaires à la reconstruction de la capitale. Cette affiche est une première tentative du British Travel and Holiday Association Board pour relancer le tourisme. La Chambre des Communes ayant été totalement détruite lors d'un bombardement en mai 1941, sa reconstruction débuta en 1950.

LAMBETH PALACE AND THE HOUSE OF COMMONS

ACRYLIC PAINTING BY ALFRED DANIELS,
RBA, RWS, ARCA, 1978

Although by the late twentieth century the Thames River had lost its significance as the means by which goods were carried to the city and as the place where ships were built, the river remains the most important and remarkable landmark of London.

Lambeth Palace on the south end of the river, home to the Archbishop of Canterbury since 1200, is the center of the Church of England. The House of Commons, on the left of the river facing east, forms part of the Houses of Parliament (rebuilt in 1852 and anchored by Big Ben) and remains the center of political power for the United Kingdom and Northern Ireland. Lambeth Bridge (built in 1861) is in the foreground and is followed by Westminster Bridge (built in 1750), Hungerford Bridge at Charing Cross (built in 1864), and Waterloo Bridge (built in 1817) in the distance at the bend of the river. Many of the famous buildings that long dominated the City of London are now overshadowed by office and apartment blocks, but can be seen clearly from the Thames because of their proximity to the river.

LAMBETH PALACE UND DAS HOUSE OF COMMONS

ACRYLMALEREI VON ALFRED DANIELS,
RBA, RWS, ARCA, 1978

Auch wenn die Themse im späten 20. Jahrhundert als Versorgungsweg für die Stadt und im Schiffsbau an Bedeutung verlor, so ist sie doch heute noch das bedeutendste und imposanteste Wahrzeichen Londons.

Der Lambeth Palace, seit 1200 die Residenz des Erzbischofs von Canterbury, liegt am Südende des Flusses und ist das Zentrum der Church of England. Das Unterhaus, links vom Fluss gelegen und nach Osten ausgerichtet, ist Teil des House of Parliament (1852 wiederaufgebaut und flankiert vom Big Ben) und heute noch das Zentrum der politischen Macht des Vereinigten Königreichs und Nordirlands. Die Lambeth Bridge (1861 erbaut) befindet sich im Vordergrund, dahinter die Westminster Bridge (1750 erbaut), die Hungerford Bridge am Charing Cross (1864 erbaut) und die Waterloo Bridge (1817 erbaut) an der Flussbiegung. Viele der berühmten Gebäude, die einst das Stadtbild Londons dominierten, werden nun von den Büro- und Wohnblöcken verdeckt, doch aufgrund ihrer Lage nahe am Fluss kann man von der Themse aus einen guten Blick auf sie werfen.

LE PALAIS DE LAMBETH ET LA CHAMBRE DES COMMUNES

ACRYLIQUE SUR TOILE D'ALFRED DANIELS,
RBA, RWS, ARCA, 1978

Même si la Tamise a perdu de son importance comme voie d'approvisionnement pour la ville et dans la construction navale à la fin du XXe siècle, c'est aujourd'hui encore l'emblème capital et le plus imposant de Londres.

Le Lambeth Palace, depuis 1200 résidence de l'archevêque de Canterbury et situé du côté sud du fleuve, est le centre de l'Église d'Angleterre (Church of England). La Chambre des Communes, à gauche du fleuve et orientée vers l'est, fait partie de la House of Parliament (reconstruite en 1852 et flanquée de Big Ben) ; aujourd'hui encore, c'est le centre du pouvoir politique du Royaume-Uni et de l'Irlande du Nord. Lambeth Bridge (construit en 1861) se trouve au premier plan, derrière vient Westminster Bridge (construit en 1750), puis les ponts de Hungerford à Charing Cross (construit en 1864) et celui de Waterloo (construit en 1817) dans le coude du fleuve. De nombreux bâtiments célèbres, qui dominaient jadis la physionomie de Londres, sont à présent masqués par des pâtés de bureaux et d'appartements, toutefois, en raison de leur proximité du fleuve, il est possible de bien les voir depuis la Tamise.

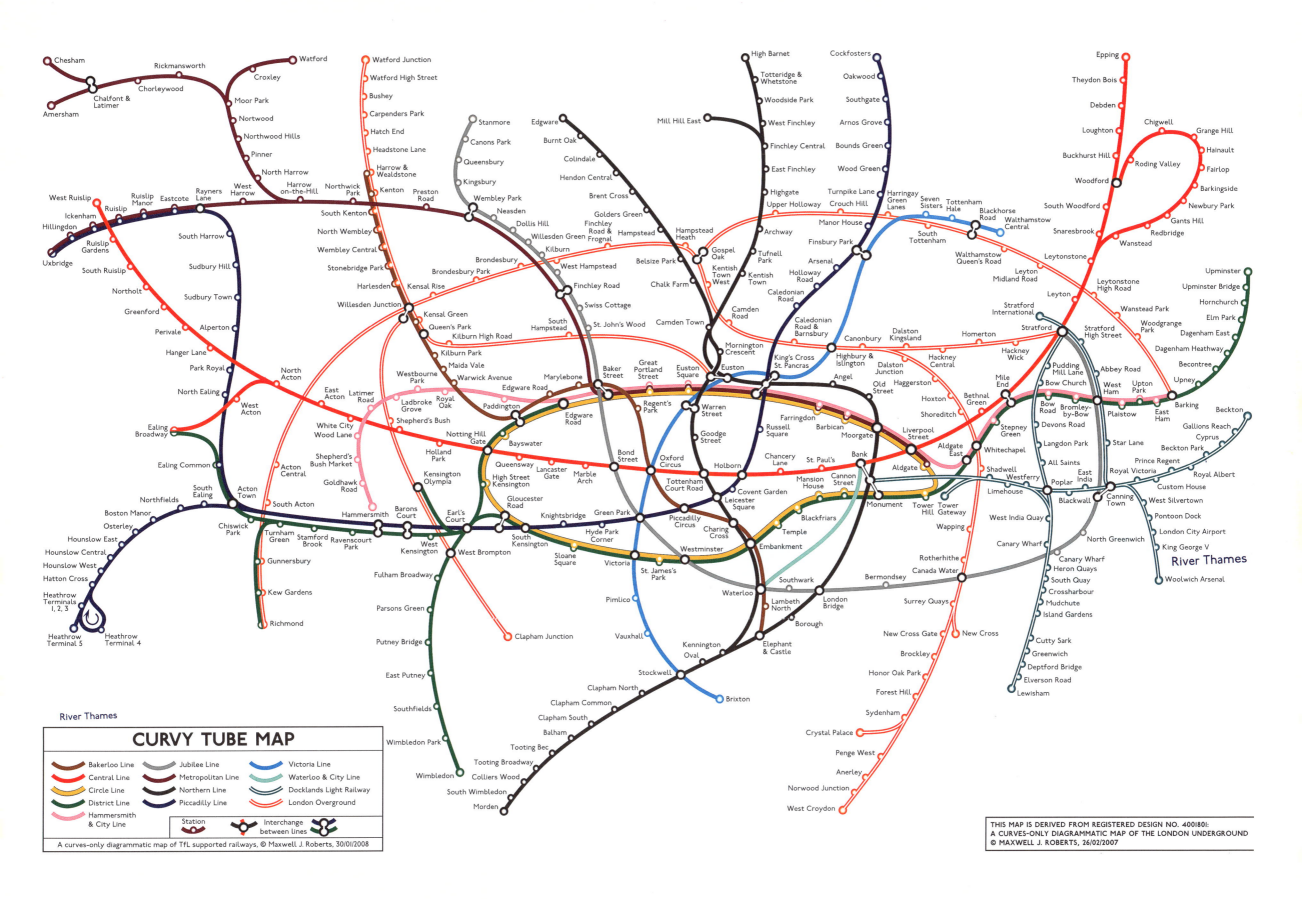

Curvy Map of the London Underground (Tube) and Docklands Light Railway

ILLUSTRATION BY MAXWELL J. ROBERTS, 2005 (AFTER BECK'S LONDON UNDERGROUND MAPS)

The Underground Service is the central artery that connects the railway and bus services. Today the Tube, as it is known, is the underground network used by most city workers and tourists to get around London, and the long, deep escalators and frequent reminders to "mind the gap" provide fond memories for visitors.

In 1933, Henry Beck's famous schematic of the London Underground was published for the first time. In Beck's map the chaotic tangle of train lines was tamed and converted into simple straightened routes, all easy to see, follow, and understand. Overnight, this powerful image transformed Londoners' perception of the Underground and their city.

Seventy-five years later many more routes have been squeezed into the Underground system, overloading the simple, powerful effect of Beck's work.

On Curvy Map the lines are shown as gentle curves, and changes in direction are smooth; much easier for the eyes to follow than sharp kinks. The result has been described as friendly, fun, and feminine, a map that many people enjoy looking at and that makes them want to travel. The illustrator, who is also a psychology professor, saw Beck's diagram as a challenge for change.

Streckenkarte der Londoner U-Bahn (Tube) und Docklands Light Railway

ILLUSTRATION VON MAXWELL J. ROBERTS, 2005 (NACH BECKS LONDONER U-BAHN KARTEN)

Die U-Bahn ist das zentrale Verkehrsmittel, das Zug- und Busdienste miteinander verbindet. Heute ist die Tube, wie die U-Bahn auch genannt wird, ein von fast allen Berufstätigen und Touristen genutztes Transportmittel in London. Die langen und tief laufenden Rolltreppen sowie die häufige Ansage »Mind the gap!« (»Vorsicht Spalt!«) bleiben Besuchern in bester Erinnerung.

1933 erschien die erste Ausgabe der berühmten schematischen Darstellung der Londoner U-Bahn von Henry Beck. Dieser bändigte das chaotische Wirrwarr der Streckenführung und stellte die Strecken einfach und übersichtlich geradlinig dar – nun waren die Karten einfach zu lesen und zu verstehen. Über Nacht wandelte sich durch diese effektive Darstellung das Bild, das die Londoner von der U-Bahn und ihrer Stadt hatten.

Innerhalb der vergangenen 75 Jahre wurden dem U-Bahnsystem immer mehr Streckenverläufe hinzugefügt, das schlichte und eindrucksvolle Werk Becks wirkte nun überladen.

Auf der neuen Karte sind die Strecken mit leicht geschwungenen Linien dargestellt, die Richtungsänderungen sind ohne Ecken und Kanten und somit viel einfacher und augenfreundlicher zu lesen als scharf abknickende Linien. Das Resultat ist eine Karte, die als freundlich, beschwingt und feminin beschrieben wird, eine Karte, die Spaß macht und Reiselust aufkommen lässt. Der Grafiker, der übrigens auch Psychologieprofessor ist, sah Becks schematische Darstellung als Herausforderung, etwas zu verändern.

Plan des correspondances du métro londonien (Tube) et du Docklands Light Railway

ILLUSTRATION DE MAXWELL J. ROBERTS, 2005 (D'APRÈS LES CARTES DE MÉTRO LONDONIEN DE BECK)

Le métro est le moyen de transport central qui relie les services ferroviaires et de bus. Actuellement, le « Tube », comme le métro est aussi appelé, est un moyen de transport en commun utilisé par presque tous les travailleurs et les touristes à Londres. Bien présents à la des visiteurs restent ses escalators interminables et l'annonce fréquente « Mind the gap! » (Attention à l'espace!).

En 1933 est parue la première édition du célèbre schéma du métro londonien par Henry Beck. Celui-ci débrouilla l'écheveau des correspondances en les représentant simplement et de façon claire par des lignes droites : les plans étaient devenus faciles à lire et compréhensibles. Du jour au lendemain, cette représentation effective changea l'image que les Londoniens se faisaient du métro et de leur ville.

Au cours des 75 dernières années, de nouvelles correspondances vinrent sans cesse s'ajouter au réseau du métro, surchargeant à présent l'œuvre sobre et impressionnante de Beck.

Sur le nouveau plan, les correspondances sont représentées par des lignes légèrement ondulées, les changements n'ont plus ni coins ni arêtes et sont ainsi plus faciles à lire et plus respectueux des yeux que les lignes s'arrêtant abruptement. Le résultat est une carte qui est décrite comme étant sympathique, en mouvement et féminine, une carte qui fait plaisir et fait naître l'envie de voyager. Le graphiste, qui est également professeur de psychologie, a considéré le schéma de Beck comme un défi visant à apporter un changement.